Evergreen Pacific

Cruising Guide

Washington Waters

Much as the early settlers viewed the way west, Pacific Northwest boaters often view the sea as a "Last Frontier." Every course planned is a new mystery to be unraveled; every voyage undertaken, a new challenge.

Aside from the romance and fun associated with the sea, good seamanship is an acquired skill involving practical experience, good sense, and pre-planning.

The original Evergreen Pacific Cruising Guide, published twenty-seven years ago, was designed to provide boaters with the navigational aids necessary to plan voyages anywhere in Washington waters. This new, revised edition continues in that same tradition with reproductions of the latest National Ocean Services charts for Washington waters, U.S. Coast Guard bar advisories, and an extensive index of sites and features.

Evergreen Pacific Cruising Guide
Copyright © 1994 by Evergreen Pacific Publishing Ltd.
18002 15th Ave. NE, Suite B • Shoreline, WA 98155

Reprinted 1995, 2000 & 2003

Cover photo: © Neil Rabinowitz 1992

ISBN 0-945265-29-8

Printed in Hong Kong

For More Evergreen Pacific Publications Visit Our Web-site:
www.evergreenpacific.com

Table of Contents

Publisher's Notes

Maintaining Up-to-Date Information on These Charts

This guide contains reproductions of the latest National Ocean Service (NOS) charts available at the time of publication. Please keep in mind, however, that most of these government charts are updated on a regular basis—some more than once a year, some every two to three years. Because natural and artificial changes, some of them critical, are constantly occurring in the areas covered by these charts, a chart may become obsolete for use for navigation. This same factor exists for any National Ocean Service charts you might purchase. We recommend that you subscribe to the **Local Notice to Mariners**. This weekly publication is free and lists all corrections to National Ocean Service charts, making it easy for you to hand-correct the important changes on the charts in this guide. Over a period of years some of your pages will acquire a number of corrections, so occasionally you will want to buy a new edition of this guide. *The Evergreen Pacific Cruising Guide* is updated every five years. You can obtain your free subscription to the **Local Notice to Mariners** by writing or calling:

Aids to Navigation
Commander Thirteenth Coast Guard District
915 Second Avenue
Seattle, WA 98174-1067
(206) 553-5864

Sites, Facilities and Services

Because of constant changes in the services marine facilities offer, we have included only the names and locations of islands, bays, harbors, passages, towns, and special sites and parks in our index on pages 4 & 5. We strongly urge Northwest boaters to purchase the annual guide edition of **Northwest Boat Travel**. This annual guide includes descriptions of over 500 sites, facilities, and services for the area covered by *The Evergreen Pacific Cruising Guide*. Our index and index locator chart are based on entries in this guide, making it a perfect companion to our atlas. **Northwest Boat Travel** is available in most marine supply stores, or you may order directly from its publisher a subscription to the annual guide (published each May) by calling **1-800-338-0804** or writing:

Anderson Publishing Company
Post Office Box 220
Anacortes, WA 98221-0220

Crossing International Boundaries

Please remember that U.S. and Canadian laws require that all foreign vessels arriving from a foreign port or place must make first landing, anchoring, or contacting of another vessel at a customs port and must report immediately to a customs officer. Boaters should be aware that Canadian law requires all ships to have on board, maintain, and use appropriate government navigational charts. Privately published charts do not satisfy this requirement.

For Those Who Enjoy Fishing

Washington waters provide excellent fishing for salmon and bottom fish. To locate those hot spots for Chinook, blackmouth, kings, silver, coho, and the several varieties of bottom fish found in this area, we recommend the **Evergreen Pacific Fishing Guide**. This guide is unique in that it supplies separate data for incoming and outgoing tides. **Please Note:** Because of the negative impact of the northern shift of the warm El Niño Current on the salmon population, restrictions on salt water fishing have increased and are subject to change at any time during the year. For the latest regulatory information, including seasons and emergency changes, call the Sport Fishing Hotline at 1-976-3200 (cost 75¢ per call). Calls from areas blocked from 976 service can be made to (206) 427-9500 (regular long distance charge).

U.S. AND CANADIAN CUSTOMS REPORTING REQUIREMENTS FOR PLEASURE VESSELS

Canadian and U.S. laws require that all foreign vessels arriving from a foreign port or place must make first landfall, or "touch" at a Customs Port. These are listed below. "Touching" consists of (1) anchoring in foreign waters; (2) coming alongside a dock in foreign waters; (3) contacting a hovering vessel. Regulations require that the Master of each vessel report immediately. The Master only is permitted to go ashore to make the report and then must return to his vessel until inspection is completed. All passengers, merchandise and baggage must be held on board until released.

If you are returning from as fishing or pleasure visit in Canadian waters and have not "touched," as defined above, you are not required to report. Custom officers may, of course, board and inspect any vessel even though a report is not required. Sport fishermen require a personal license in B.C. tidal waters.

Before you leave on your trip to foreign waters, it would be helpful to obtain the telephone number of the Customs office nearest to your anticipated port of return in the United States or Canada. The Customs officer will be pleased to offer you information and assistance on reporting requirements as well as other general Customs information, including pamphlets.

Custom Phone Numbers

Customs officials work on a 24-hour basis, but should be called the day before if arrival will be other than regular working hours. An asterisk * denotes ports which have extended hours of service. United States Customs Service has a toll free number for Sundays and holidays, and nights 5 p.m. to 8 a.m.: 1-800-552-5943.

United States		Canada	
Aberdeen	532-2030	Banfield	728-3388
Anacortes	293-2331	Bedwell (May-Oct.)	629-3363
Bellingham	734-5463	Campbell River	287-3761
Blaine	332-5771	Courtney (Comox)	334-3424
Everett	259-0246	Kitimat	632-7611
Friday Harbor	378-2080	Nanaimo	754-0341
(Roche Harbor)		Port Alberni	723-6612
Neah Bay	645-2312	Powell River	485-2243
Olympia (Tacoma)	593-6336	Prince Rupert	627-3003
Port Angeles	457-4311	Sidney *	356-6645 or 356-6644
Port Townsend	385-3777	Stewart	636-2483
Pt. Roberts	945-2314	Ucluelet	726-4241
Seattle	442-4678	Vancouver*	666-0272,
South Bend – Raymond	532-2030		666-0273 or 666-0274
(Aberdeen)		Victoria *	388-3339 or 388-3330
Tacoma	593-6336		

VISUAL DISTRESS SIGNALS

The following chart gives the various types of visual distress signals available:

NUMBER MARKED ON DEVICE	DESCRIPTION	APPROVED FOR USE DURING:	OPTIMUM CONDITIONS FOR USE:
160.022	Floating Orange Smoke Distress Signals (5 minutes)	Day	Clear, Light Wind
160.037	Hand held Orange Smoke Distress Signals	Day	Clear, Light Wind
160.057	Floating Orange Smoke Distress Signals (15 minutes)	Day	Clear, Light Wind
160.072	Orange Distress Signal Flag for Boats	Day	Bright Sunlight
161.072	Electric Distress Light for Boats	Night	Within sight of shore or other boats
160.21	Hand held Flare Distress Signal (Dated after November 30, 1980)	Day & Night	Night or Foggy Day
160.24	Parachute Red Flare Distress Signals 37mm (Must also carry suitable launcher)	Day & Night	Light Wind
160.036	Hand held Rocket-Propelled Parachute Red Flare Distress Signals	Day & Night	Light Wind
160.066	Distress Signal for Boats, Red Aerial Pyrotechnic flare (parachute) – launcher sometimes required	Day & Night	Light Wind
160.066	Distress Signal for Boats, Red Aerial Pyrotechnic Flare (meteor) – launcher sometimes required	Day & Night	Squalls, Heavy Wind

A flare can only be used once, so use it wisely. If on the open sea, use a flare when another boat or a plane is within earshot. If signalling to shore, look for signs of people, such as lights or houses, before using flares. Remember that flares have a short burn time: hand-held flares, two minutes; aerial, ten seconds.

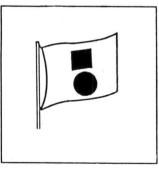

The approved orange distress flag must measure at least 3 x 3 feet and consist of a black square above a black ball agasinst an orange background. The flag is most distinctive when waived on a paddle or boathook or flown from a mast. When signalling to a plane, lay the flag flat over a cabin top.

Pyrotechnic distress signals should be stored in a cool, dry place that is easily reached in an emergency. Flares with a punctured or otherwise damaged covering may not work. The U.S. Coast Guard recommends storage in a watertight container such as a surplus ammunition box, painted red or orange and prominently marked "Distress Signals."

Handle pyrotechnic signals with care; projected signals, such as parachute flares and meteors, have characteristics similar to a firearm and should be treated with the same respect.

The hand-held devices have a very hot flame and usually give off ash and slag that can cause burns and start fires. When burning a flare, hold the device over the side of the boat in such a way that slag will not drip onto the hand.

1

Aids for Boaters

BRIDGE CLEARANCES AND SIGNALS
Canada (in meters)
Contact bridge tender on VHF 12, or signal with three long blasts with following exceptions. All bridges closed between midnight and 6:00 A.M. LLW: Lowest Low Water. HHW: Highest High Water. When no height is given, clearance in most cases is extremely low.

Fraser River
Annacis Ch. East Bridge 12.2M LLW
Annacis Ch. Swing Bridge 6.0M LLW
Alex Fraser Bridge 61.1M LLW
B.C. Hydro Rail Bridge — — —
Deas Slough Causeway 2.4M HHW
N.W.R.R. Bridge 9.6M LLW
Pattullo Bridge 47.0M LLW
Pitt River Hwy. Bridge 6.1M HHW - — — —
Pitt River Rail Bridge 3.35M HHW
Port Mann Bridge 48.2M LLW
Westham Is. Bridge
B.C. Transit Bridge
Queensborough Bridge 27.1M LLW

Main Stem
Purfleet Pt. 53M HHW
Below Gunderson Slough 56M HHW
Above Leeder Avenue 43M HHW

Annacis Channel
Purfleet Pt. 24M HHW
Patrick Is. 30M HHW

Pitt River
Downriver of Lougheed Hwy. 36.8M HHW
Downriver of MacIntyre Creek 24.4M HHW

Parsons Channel
192nd St. 24.4M HHW

United States (in feet)
Heights are in feet above Mean High Water.
Short blast – 1 second; long blast – 4-5 seconds

La Conner, Swinomish Channel
Burlington Northern RR 7.7; Freeway 75.7'
*Drawbridge 16.3' down; 79.3' up — —
Rainbow South Bridge 75.9'; Power cables 72'

Hood Canal
*Draw section of Bridge: opens on signal with at least one hour's notice. One can also call the Seattle Marine Operator Station KOTT or (206) 779-3377.
Fixed East Span 55'; Fixed West Span 35'

Seattle, Canal and Lake Washington
*Gt. Northern RR 43' — —
Canal Locks — — — —
Canal Locks with tow — — — — —
Ballard 29' (46' under center of span) — —
Fremont Ave. 30' (under the 100' horizontal span) — —
University 29' (46' under center of span) — — — —
Montlake 30' (46' under horizontal 63' span) — —
Evergreen Floating Bridge (Foster Is. to Evergreen Pt.) — — —
  Fixed East Span 57'; Fixed West Span 44'
Mercer Island Floating Bridge — —
  East and West fixed spans 31' min., 38' max.
Mercer Island (East side of island) 65' Fixed

Seattle, Duwamish and West Waterway
*2 Spokane St. Highway Bridges 24' (43' at center) and Burlington R.R. Bridge 8'
Signal opens all three bridges — — — —
Burlington R.R. only — —
1st Ave. So. 24' (41' at center) — — —
14th Ave. So. 21' (34' at center) — — —

Tacoma, City Waterway
So. 11th St. Highway Bridge: 64' down, 139' up — —
Union Pacific near So. 15th St. 6' — — —

Tacoma, Puyallup Waterway
E. 11th St. 29' when fixed; 138' up
E. 11th R.R. 12' down
Open on 24-hour notice — — — — —

Tacoma, Port Industrial (Blair) Waterway
*E. 11th St. 8' at center — —

Tacoma, Hylebos Waterway
*E. 11th St. 21' at center — —

Hale Passage
Fox Island Bridge 31' at center Fixed

Carr Inlet, Henderson Bay
Raft Island Bridge 17' Fixed
Purdy Bridge 12' (23' at center) Fixed

Case Inlet
Stretch Island Bridge 14' Fixed
Reach Island Bridge 16' Fixed

*Equipped with radio phone, Channels 13 & 16.

SYMBOLS AND ABBREVIATIONS

Navigation aids:

Light (On fixed structure)   ◯ Landmark   ◎ R. Bn. radiobeacon

DFS distance finding station   △ Bn daybeacon   AERO. aeronautical

Unlighted buoy (C. can, N. nun, S. spar, Bell, Gong, Horn, Whistle)

Danger or junction buoy   Mid-channel buoy   Fish trap buoy

Lighted buoy   Anchorage buoy   Mooring buoy

Light characteristics: (Lights are white unless otherwise indicated.)

F. fixed	I. Qk. interrupted quick	G. green	M. nautical miles
Fl. flashing	E. Int. equal interval	R. red	DIA. diaphone
Gp. group	Occ. occulting	m. minutes	WHIS. whistle
Alt. alternating	Mo. (A) morse code	sec. seconds	OBSC. obscured
Qk. quick	Rot. rotating	ft. feet	SEC. sector

Bottom characteristics:

Cl. clay	M. mud	Oys oyster	stk. sticky	gn. green
Co. coral	Rk. rock	hrd. hard	bk. black	gy. gray
G. gravel	S. sand	rky. rocky	br. brown	wh. white
Grs. grass	Sh. shells	sft. soft	bu. blue	yl. yellow

Dangers:

⋅⊹⋅ Sunken wreck   ◣ Visible wreck   + ⋅ ⋅ Rocks

21 Wreck, rock, obstruction, or shoal swept clear to the depth indicated

(2) Rocks that cover and uncover, with heights in feet above datum of soundings

AUTH. authorized; Obstr. obstruction; P.A. position approximate; E.D. existence doubtful

⊛ Launching ramps   ✵ Marine parks

PERSON OVERBOARD

Boat operators who have had a passenger fall overboard report that it was much harder to perform the rescue than they ever imagined. Fatigue, surprise, fear and often alcohol make simple tasks and quick thinking difficult.

Almost all the overboard victims who died (from drowning, heart attack or hypothermia) were NOT WEARING A PERSONAL FLOATATION DEVICE and fell from a vessel whose skipper had considerable boating experience but HAD NEVER TAKEN A BOATING SAFETY COURSE.

These are general rules to recover someone who has fallen overboard. Common sense applied to a specific rescue operation may dictate a variation in this sequence of events. NOTE: Sailboat skippers face the choice of whether to attempt the rescue under sail-power or to take the time to switch to engine-power. There is no hard and fast rule. The decision must be made on the spot considering such factors as wind, sea, maneuvering room, crew competence, time available, etc. There is no substitute for a boating safety education coupled with experience (practice rescue maneuvers) and a COOL HEAD in an emergency.

1) Even if the victim is a good swimmer, throw a lifesaving device ALONGSIDE, not at, the person in the water. If a Type IV (throwable) PFD is not available, then throw anything that will provide floatation.
2) Keep the victim in view. Appoint a passenger to act as look out and, at night, shine a light on the victim.
   NOTE: In three out of four recreational boat drownings, the victim disappeared within FIVE MINUTES of entering the water.
3) When close enough to extend the victim a short line, paddle or towel, STOP THE ENGINE and lead the person around to the stern of the boat.
4) Help the victim aboard. If it is necessary for someone to go into the water to assist the overboard victim get back into the boat, that person should wear a PFD and tether himself to the boat.
5) Make the victim as warm and dry as possible. If the victim was in the water for over 15 minutes the person is probably suffering some degree of hypothermia, in which case DO NOT administer hot drinks or alcohol and seek medical help at once.

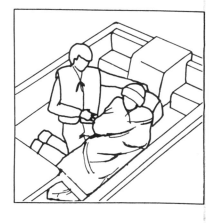

Dry the victim and protect from further heat loss. Note head covering.

Aids for Boaters

WEATHER

Storm Warnings

Small Craft Warning: Winds forecast up to 33 knots and/or sea conditions dangerous to small crafts.
Gale Warning: Winds forecast from 34-47 knots.
Storm Warning: Winds forecast from 48-63 knots.
Hurricane Warning: Winds forecast 64 knots and above.

Before Leaving

1. Check weather report for period of trip — postpone voyage if inclement weather is predicted.
2. Just in case, ensure your craft and passengers are prepared for worse weather than forecasted.
3. File a Float Plan.

While Underway Watch For

1. Gathering clouds
2. Change in wind speed and/or direction
3. Temperature change
4. Other boats returning home

If Caught in Bad Weather

1. All aboard put on PFD's (Personal Floatation Devices)
2. Switch on lights
3. Radio position
4. Reduce speed
5. Head for the nearest harbor — "Any port in a storm"
6. Ready emergency equipment

If Boat Takes on Water and Can't Make Headway

1. Don't try to out-run the storm, ride it out.
2. Head bow into waves
3. Drop anchor OR
4. Throw a bucket and line off the bow to make a sea anchor. NEVER ANCHOR OFF THE STERN

RIGHT-OF-WAY
The Giving-Way Vessel

To determine whether you should give way to another vessel, divide your horizon into three arcs relative to your course. You must give way to any vessel approaching from within the starboard arc, except to an overtaking vessel which has moved into that arc from the overtaking arc. You do not give way to any vessel approaching from within the port arc. All vessels approaching you from within the overtaking arc keep clear of you. It should be borne in mind that where risk of collision exists the vessel which has right-of-way must not alter course, or increase or reduce speed, except to avoid navigational dangers or to take avoiding action if a collision appears probable. A vessel's course is deemed to be the course which she is endeavoring to steer, and due allowance must be made by the giving-way vessel for any yawing caused by weather or other circumstances.

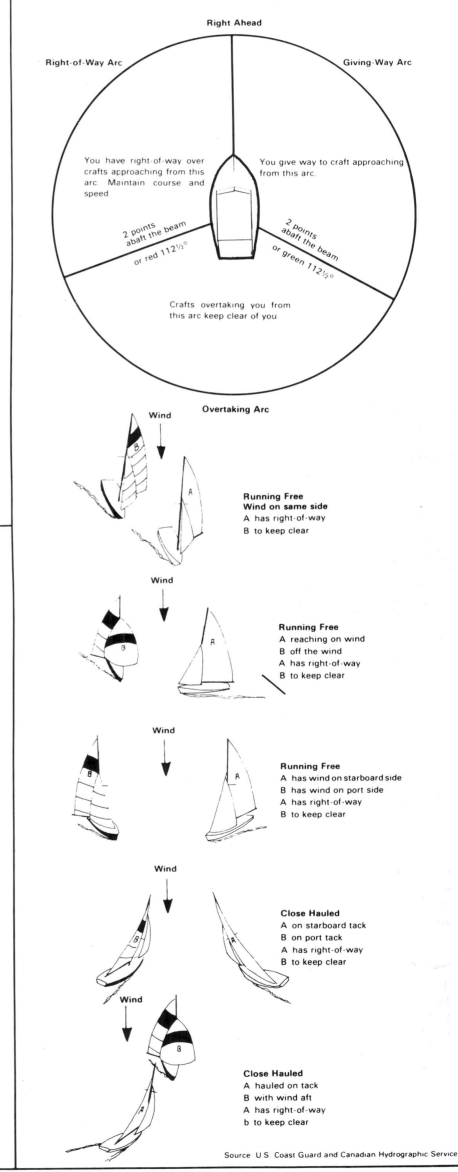

Source U.S. Coast Guard and Canadian Hydrographic Service

Index of Islands, Bays, Harbors, Passages, Towns, and Special Sites and Parks

Grid references (in parentheses) apply only to area charts. The **first** page number listed is the area chart that applies to the grid reference. Following page numbers are to large-scale, detailed charts that also contain the listed location. Not all items included in this index are listed on the NOS charts reproduced in this cruising guide. For precise directions for finding those locations, please consult *Northwest Boat Travel*.

Grid references (in parentheses) apply only to area charts. The **first** page number listed is the area chart that applies to the grid reference. Following page numbers are to large-scale, detailed charts that also contain the listed location. Not all items included in this index are listed on the NOS charts reproduced in this cruising guide. For precise directions for finding those locations, please consult *Northwest Boat Travel*.

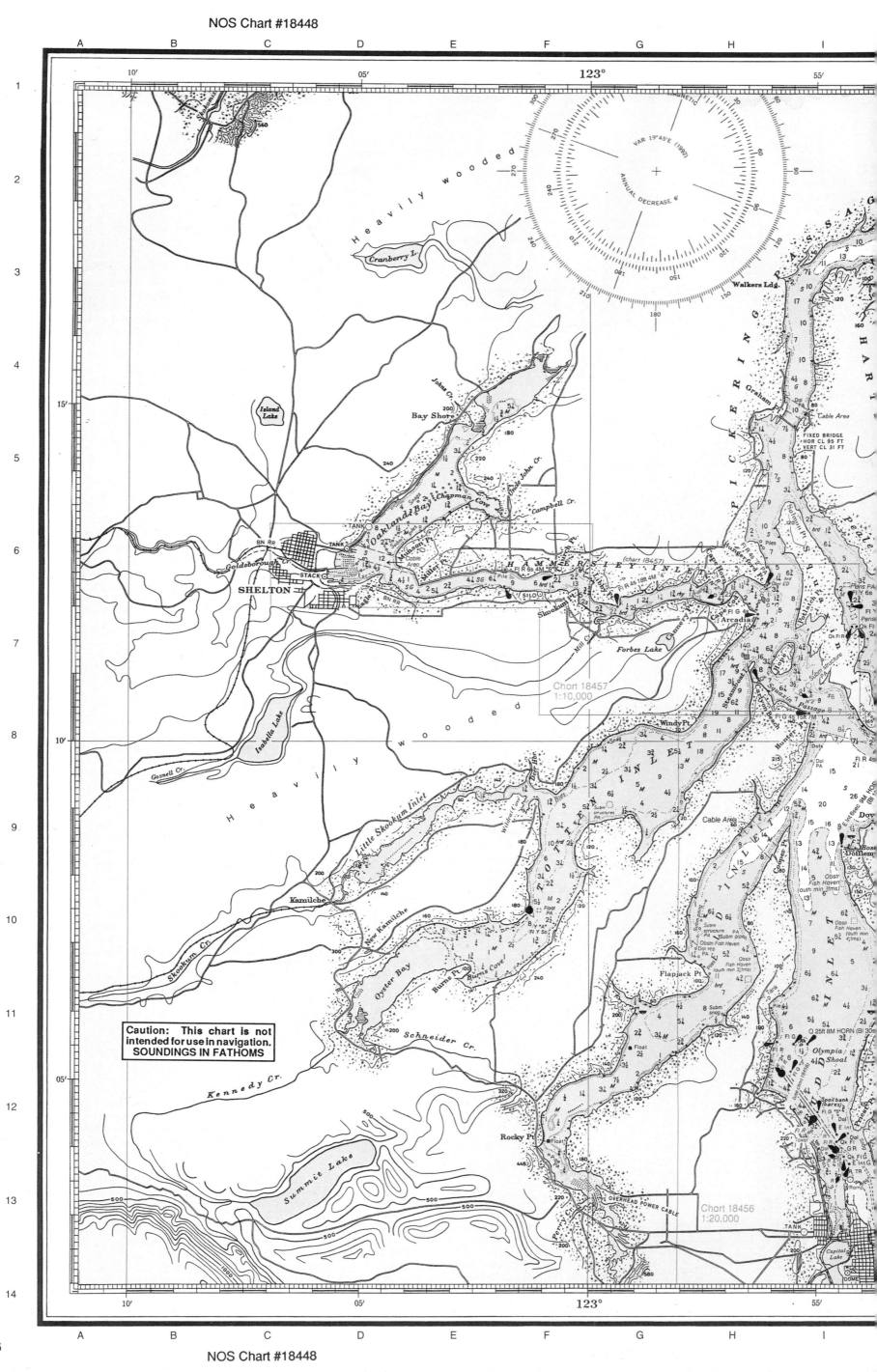

Caution: This chart is not
intended for use in navigation.
SOUNDINGS IN FATHOMS

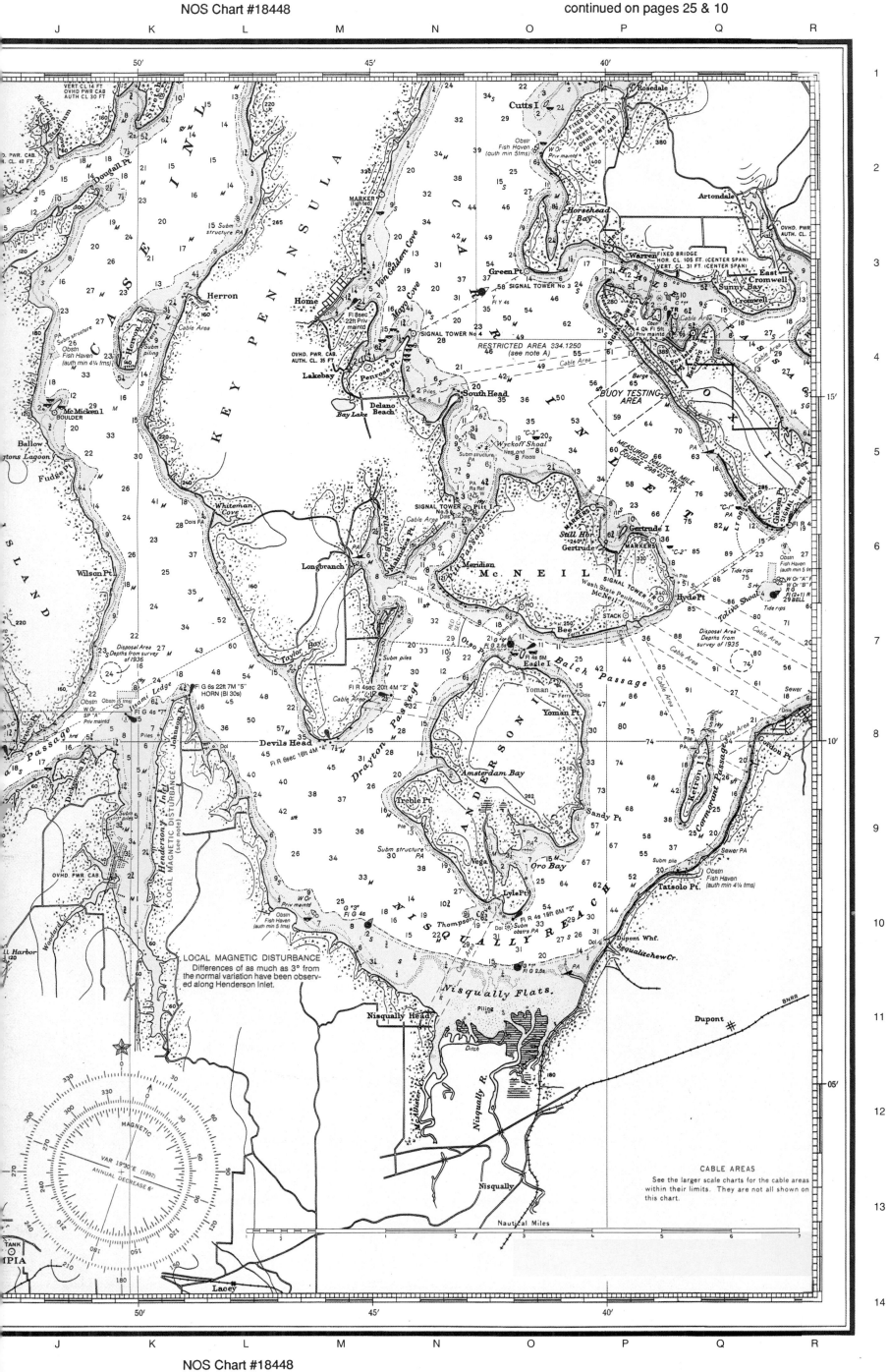

continued on page 8

LOCAL MAGNETIC DISTURBANCE
Differences of as much as 3° from
the normal variation have been observed along Henderson Inlet.

CABLE AREAS
See the larger scale charts for the cable areas
within their limits. They are not all shown on
this chart.

continued on page 10

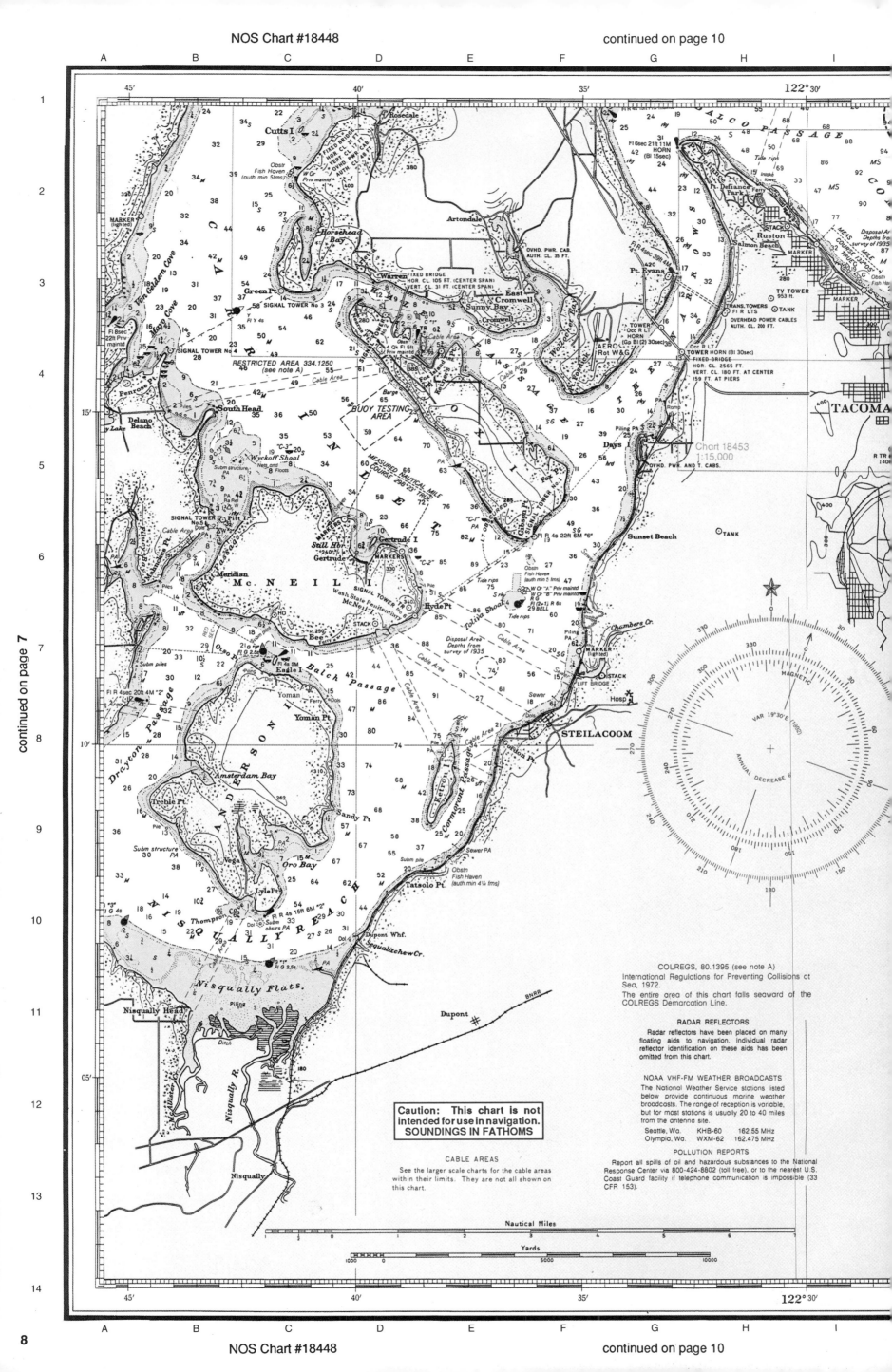

continued on page 10

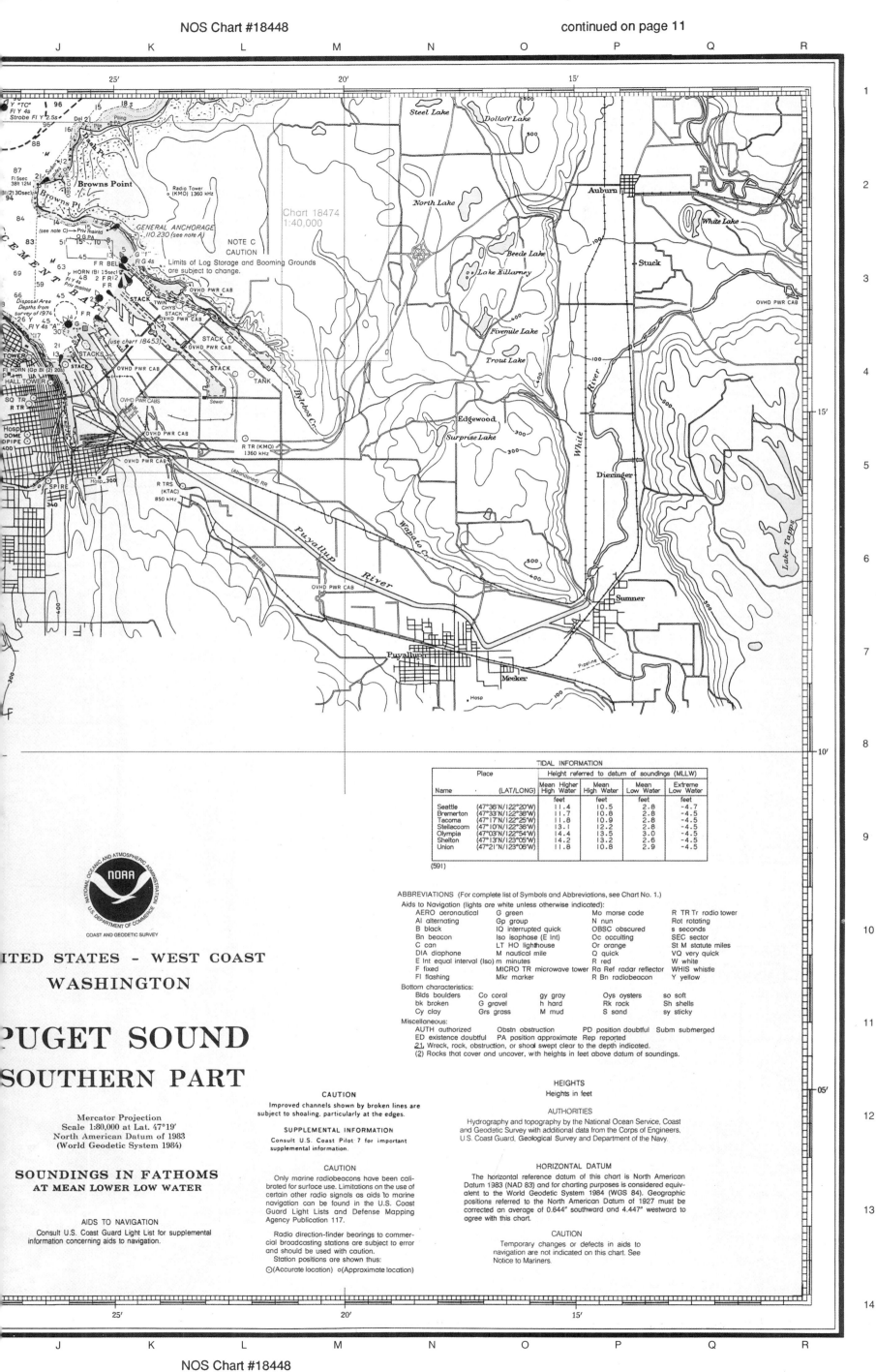

continued on page 11

TIDAL INFORMATION

	Place		Height referred to datum of soundings (MLLW)			
Name	(LAT/LONG)		Mean Higher High Water	Mean High Water	Mean Low Water	Extreme Low Water
			feet	feet	feet	feet
Seattle	(47°36'N/122°20'W)		11.4	10.5	2.8	-4.7
Bremerton	(47°33'N/122°38'W)		11.7	10.8	2.8	-4.5
Tacoma	(47°17'N/122°25'W)		11.8	10.9	2.8	-4.5
Stellacoom	(47°10'N/122°36'W)		13.1	12.2	2.8	-4.5
Olympia	(47°03'N/122°54'W)		14.4	13.5	3.0	-4.5
Shelton	(47°13'N/123°05'W)		14.2	13.2	2.6	-4.5
Union	(47°21'N/123°06'W)		11.8	10.8	2.9	-4.5

(591)

ABBREVIATIONS (For complete list of Symbols and Abbreviations, see Chart No. 1.)
Aids to Navigation (lights are white unless otherwise indicated):

AERO aeronautical	G green	Mo morse code	R TR Tr radio tower
Al alternating	Gp group	N nun	Rot rotating
B black	IQ interrupted quick	OBSC obscured	s seconds
Bn beacon	Iso isophase (E Int)	Oc occulting	SEC sector
C can	LT HO lighthouse	Or orange	St M statute miles
DIA diaphone	M nautical mile	Q quick	VQ very quick
E Int equal interval (Iso)	m minutes	R red	W white
F fixed	MICRO TR microwave tower	Ra Ref radar reflector	WHIS whistle
Fl flashing	Mkr marker	R Bn radiobeacon	Y yellow

Bottom characteristics:

Blds boulders	Co coral	gy gray	Oys oysters	so soft
bk broken	G gravel	h hard	Rk rock	Sh shells
Cy clay	Grs grass	M mud	S sand	sy sticky

Miscellaneous:

AUTH authorized   Obstn obstruction   PD position doubtful   Subm submerged
ED existence doubtful   PA position approximate   Rep reported
21, Wreck, rock, obstruction, or shoal swept clear to the depth indicated.
(2) Rocks that cover and uncover, with heights in feet above datum of soundings.

COAST AND GEODETIC SURVEY

ITED STATES – WEST COAST

WASHINGTON

PUGET SOUND

SOUTHERN PART

Mercator Projection
Scale 1:80,000 at Lat. 47°19'
North American Datum of 1983
(World Geodetic System 1984)

SOUNDINGS IN FATHOMS
AT MEAN LOWER LOW WATER

AIDS TO NAVIGATION
Consult U.S. Coast Guard Light List for supplemental
information concerning aids to navigation.

CAUTION
Improved channels shown by broken lines are
subject to shoaling, particularly at the edges.

SUPPLEMENTAL INFORMATION
Consult U.S. Coast Pilot 7 for important
supplemental information.

CAUTION
Only marine radiobeacons have been calibrated for surface use. Limitations on the use of
certain other radio signals as aids to marine
navigation can be found in the U.S. Coast
Guard Light Lists and Defense Mapping
Agency Publication 117.

Radio direction-finder bearings to commercial broadcasting stations are subject to error
and should be used with caution.
Station positions are shown thus:
⊙(Accurate location) o(Approximate location)

HEIGHTS
Heights in feet

AUTHORITIES
Hydrography and topography by the National Ocean Service, Coast
and Geodetic Survey with additional data from the Corps of Engineers,
U.S. Coast Guard, Geological Survey and Department of the Navy.

HORIZONTAL DATUM
The horizontal reference datum of this chart is North American
Datum 1983 (NAD 83) and for charting purposes is considered equivalent to the World Geodetic System 1984 (WGS 84). Geographic
positions referred to the North American Datum of 1927 must be
corrected an average of 0.644" southward and 4.447" westward to
agree with this chart.

CAUTION
Temporary changes or defects in aids to
navigation are not indicated on this chart. See
Notice to Mariners.

continued on page 14

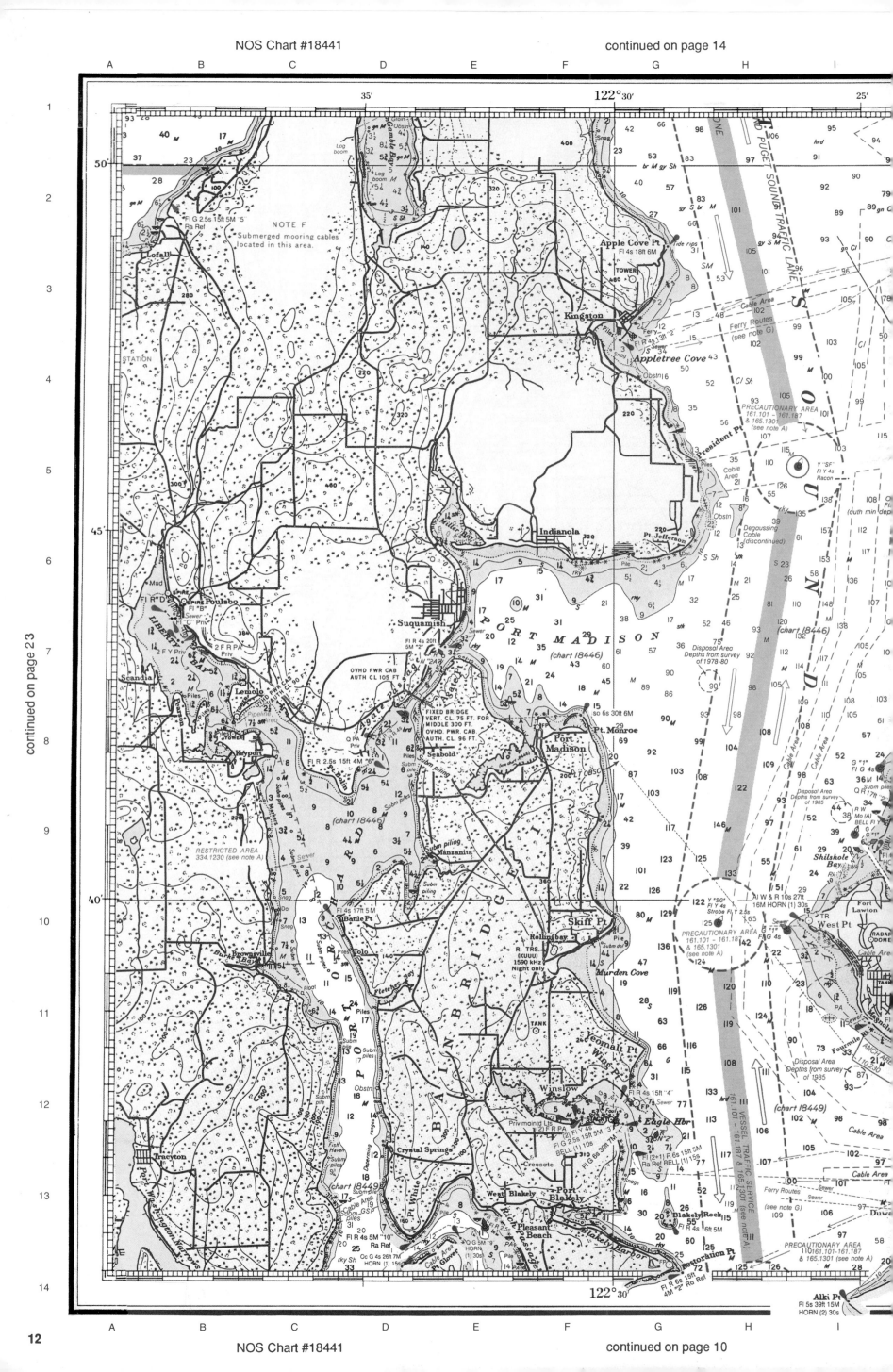

continued on page 23

continued on page 10

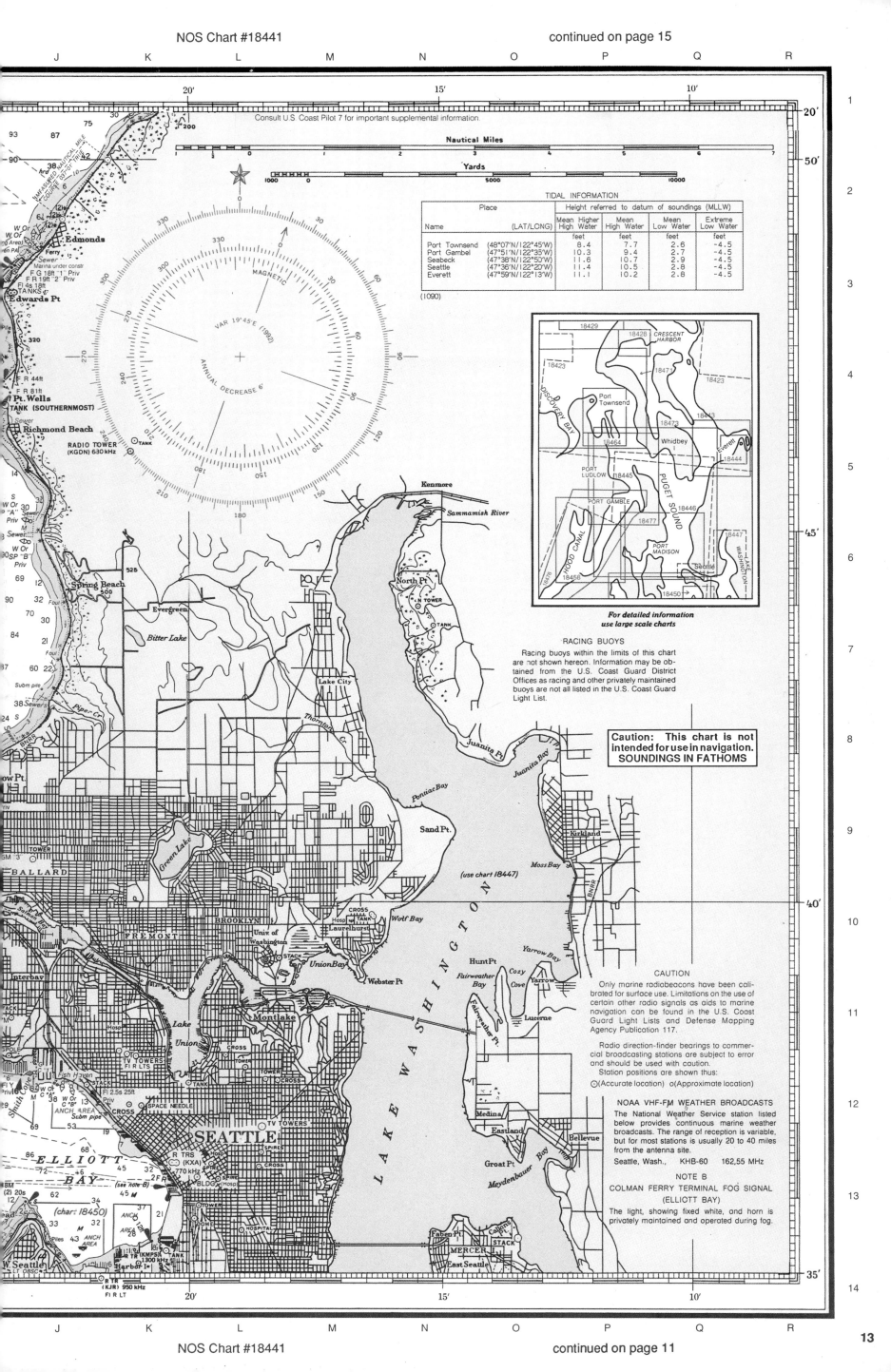

Consult U.S. Coast Pilot 7 for important supplemental information.

TIDAL INFORMATION

Place		Height referred to datum of soundings (MLLW)			
Name	(LAT/LONG)	Mean Higher High Water	Mean High Water	Mean Low Water	Extreme Low Water
		feet	feet	feet	feet
Port Townsend	(48°07'N/122°45'W)	8.4	7.7	2.6	-4.5
Port Gamble	(47°51'N/122°35'W)	10.3	9.4	2.7	-4.5
Seabeck	(47°38'N/122°50'W)	11.6	10.7	2.9	-4.5
Seattle	(47°36'N/122°20'W)	11.4	10.5	2.8	-4.5
Everett	(47°59'N/122°13'W)	11.1	10.2	2.8	-4.5

(1090)

For detailed information use large scale charts

RACING BUOYS

Racing buoys within the limits of this chart are not shown hereon. Information may be obtained from the U.S. Coast Guard District Offices as racing and other privately maintained buoys are not all listed in the U.S. Coast Guard Light List.

Caution: This chart is not intended for use in navigation. SOUNDINGS IN FATHOMS

CAUTION

Only marine radiobeacons have been calibrated for surface use. Limitations on the use of certain other radio signals as aids to marine navigation can be found in the U.S. Coast Guard Light Lists and Defense Mapping Agency Publication 117.

Radio direction-finder bearings to commercial broadcasting stations are subject to error and should be used with caution.

Station positions are shown thus:

⊙(Accurate location) o(Approximate location)

NOAA VHF-FM WEATHER BROADCASTS

The National Weather Service station listed below provides continuous marine weather broadcasts. The range of reception is variable, but for most stations is usually 20 to 40 miles from the antenna site.

Seattle, Wash., KHB-60   162.55 MHz

NOTE B
COLMAN FERRY TERMINAL FOG SIGNAL (ELLIOTT BAY)

The light, showing fixed white, and horn is privately maintained and operated during fog.

continued on page 16

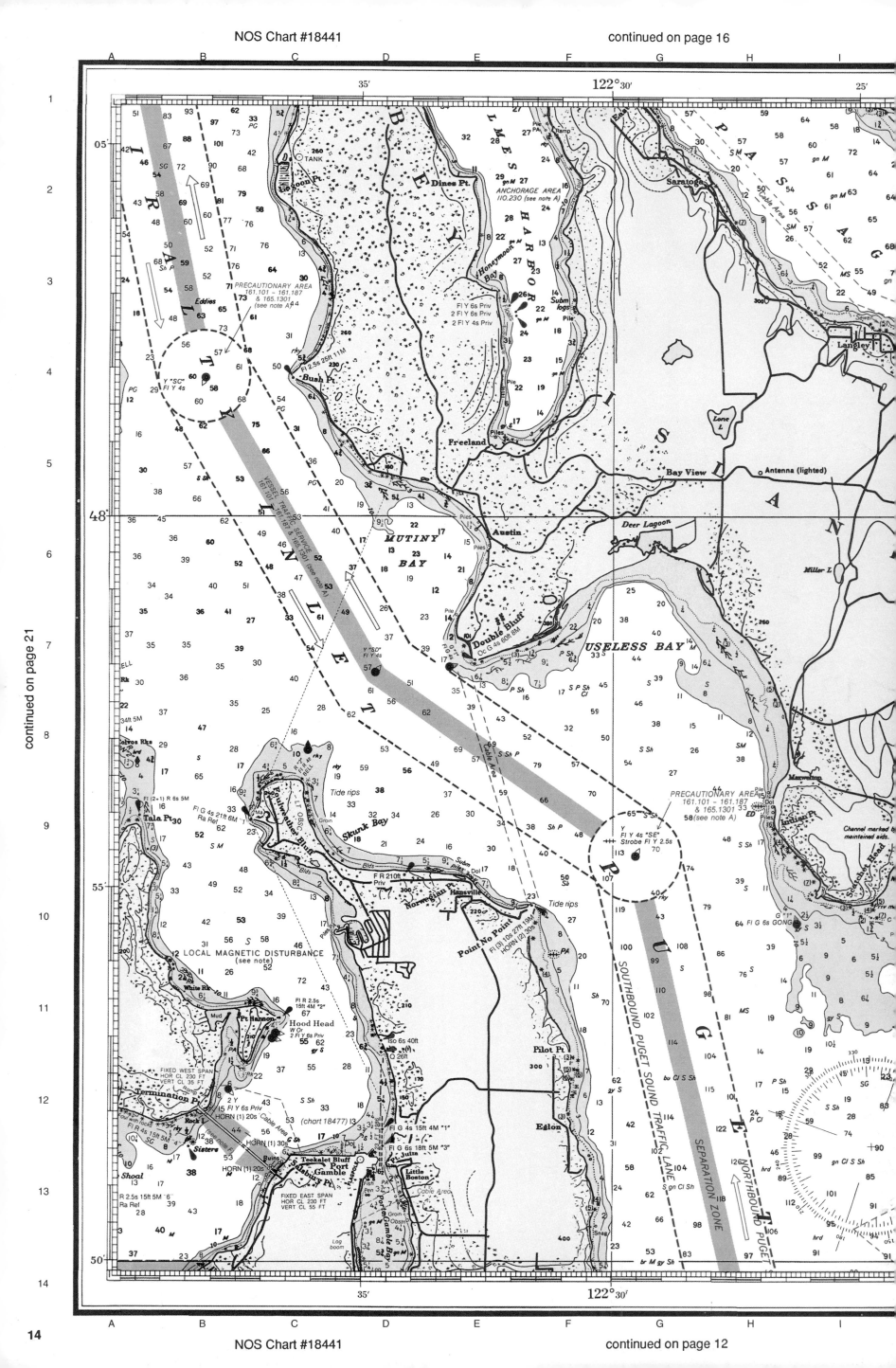

continued on page 12

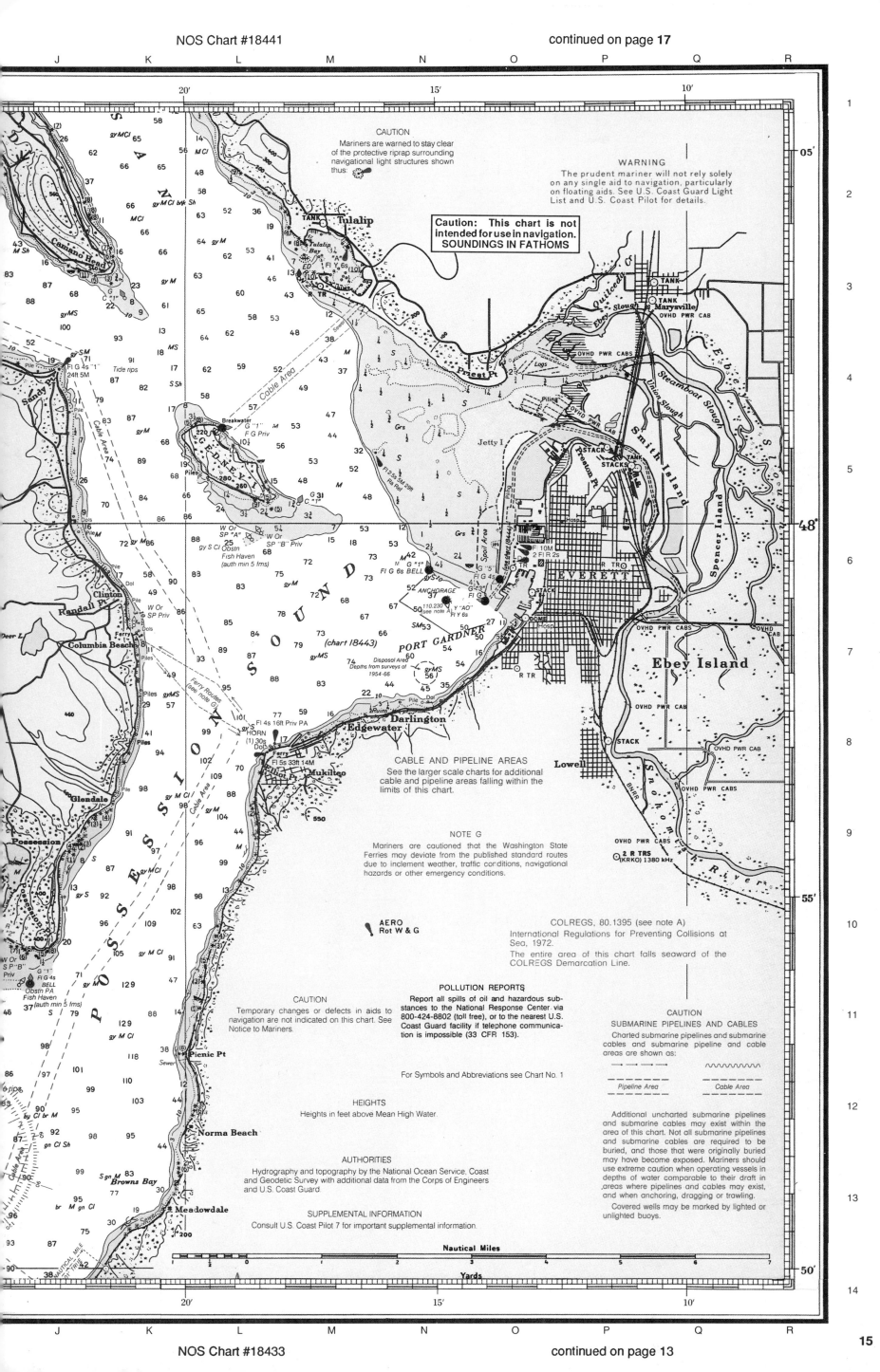

continued on page 27

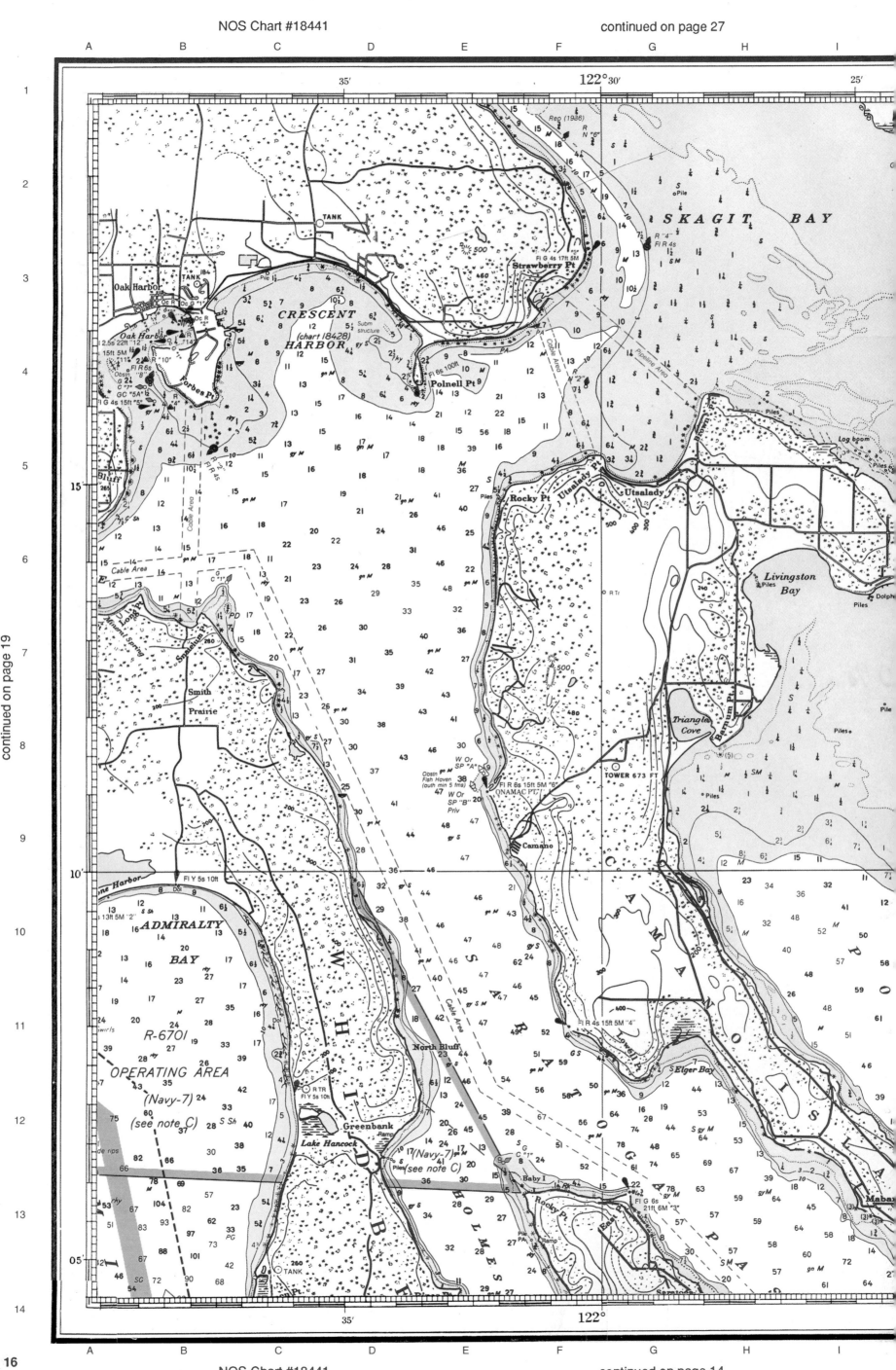

continued on page 19

continued on page 14

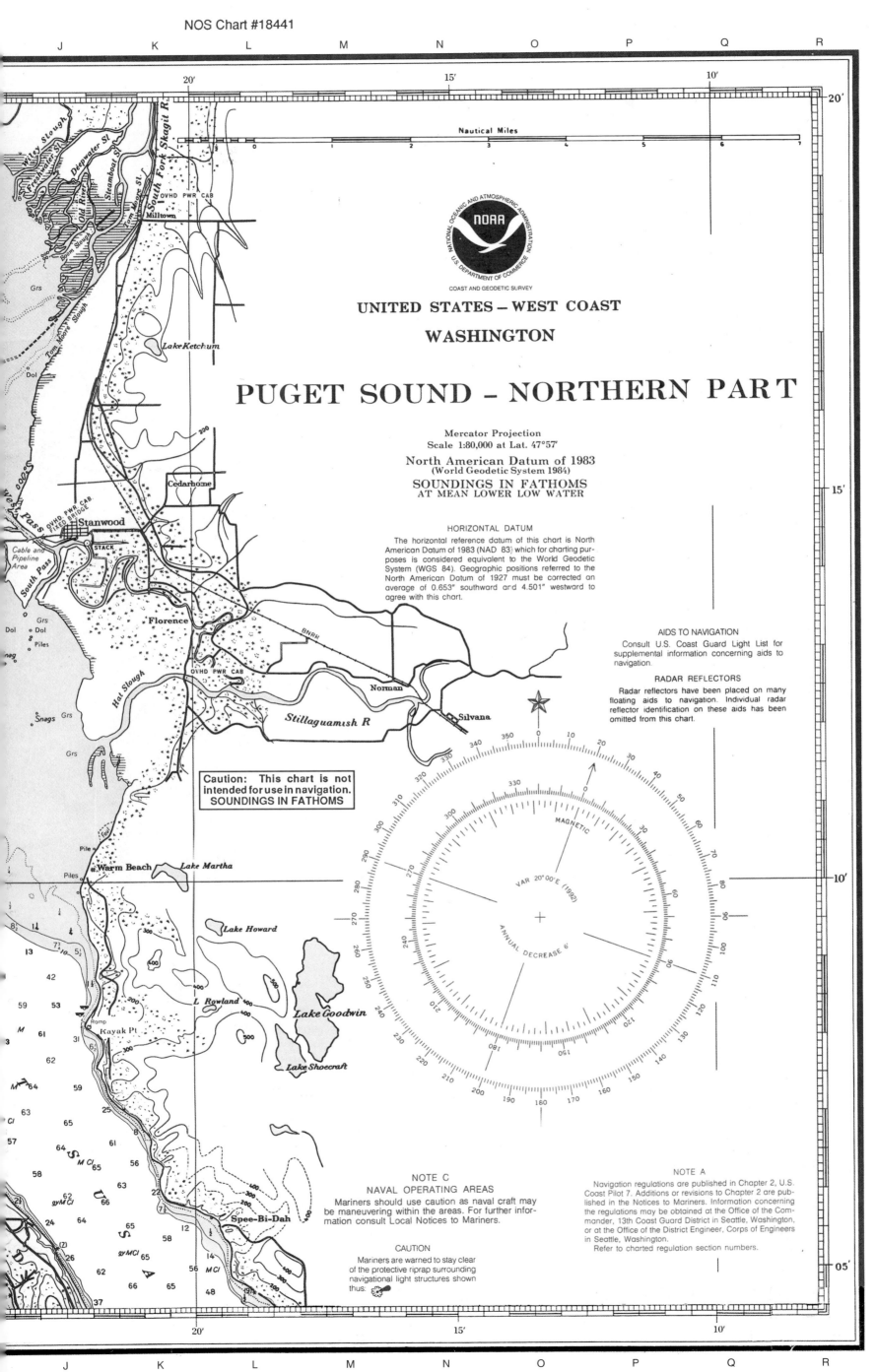

UNITED STATES — WEST COAST

WASHINGTON

PUGET SOUND – NORTHERN PART

Mercator Projection
Scale 1:80,000 at Lat. 47°57'

North American Datum of 1983
(World Geodetic System 1984)
SOUNDINGS IN FATHOMS
AT MEAN LOWER LOW WATER

HORIZONTAL DATUM

The horizontal reference datum of this chart is North American Datum of 1983 (NAD 83) which for charting purposes is considered equivalent to the World Geodetic System (WGS 84). Geographic positions referred to the North American Datum of 1927 must be corrected an average of 0.653" southward and 4.501" westward to agree with this chart.

AIDS TO NAVIGATION

Consult U.S. Coast Guard Light List for supplemental information concerning aids to navigation.

RADAR REFLECTORS

Radar reflectors have been placed on many floating aids to navigation. Individual radar reflector identification on these aids has been omitted from this chart.

Caution: This chart is not intended for use in navigation.
SOUNDINGS IN FATHOMS

NOTE C
NAVAL OPERATING AREAS

Mariners should use caution as naval craft may be maneuvering within the areas. For further information consult Local Notices to Mariners.

CAUTION

Mariners are warned to stay clear of the protective riprap surrounding navigational light structures shown thus:

NOTE A

Navigation regulations are published in Chapter 2, U.S. Coast Pilot 7. Additions or revisions to Chapter 2 are published in the Notices to Mariners. Information concerning the regulations may be obtained at the Office of the Commander, 13th Coast Guard District in Seattle, Washington, or at the Office of the District Engineer, Corps of Engineers in Seattle, Washington.
Refer to charted regulation section numbers.

continued on page 15

17

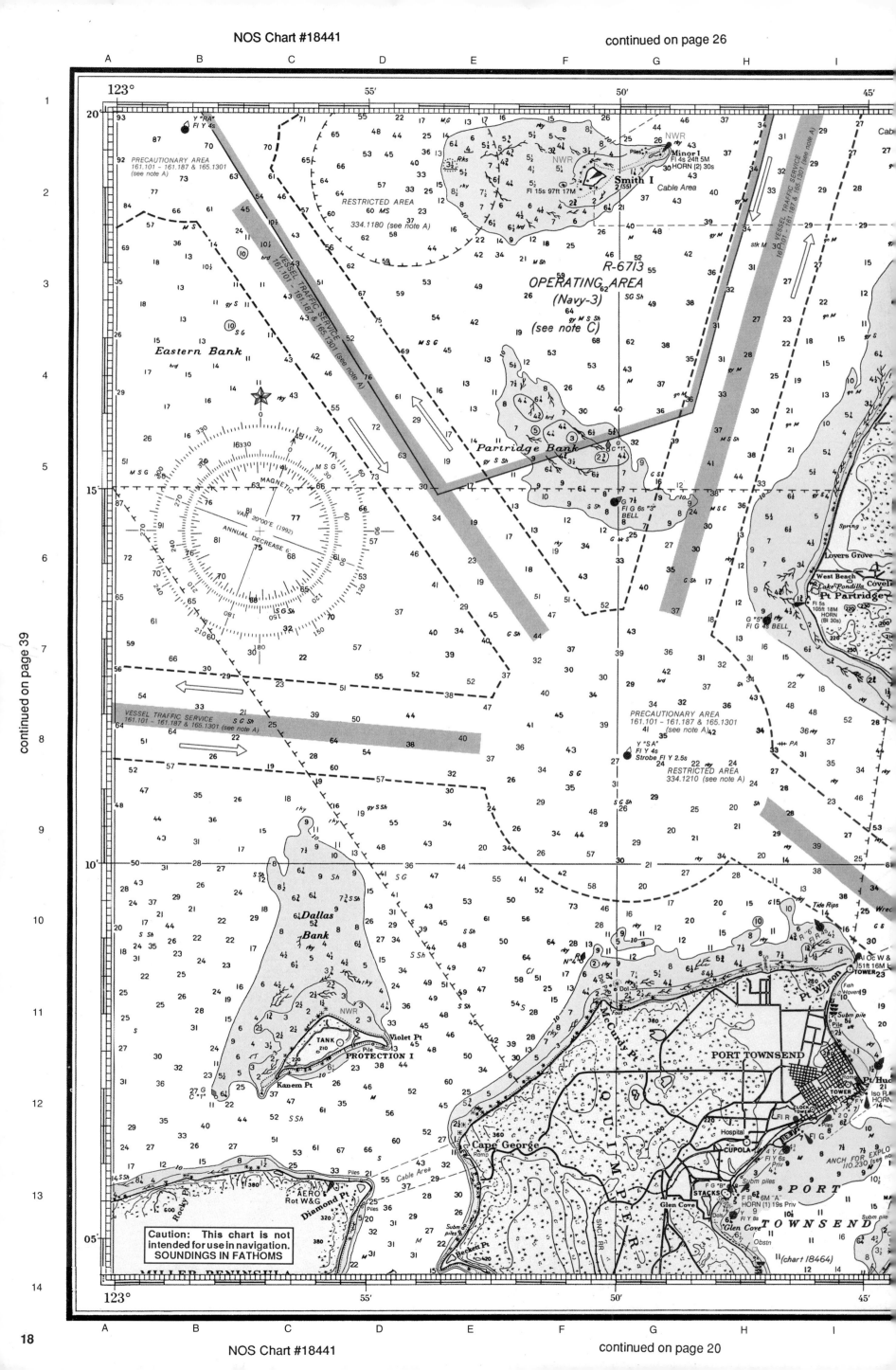

continued on page 39

continued on page 20

continued on page 27

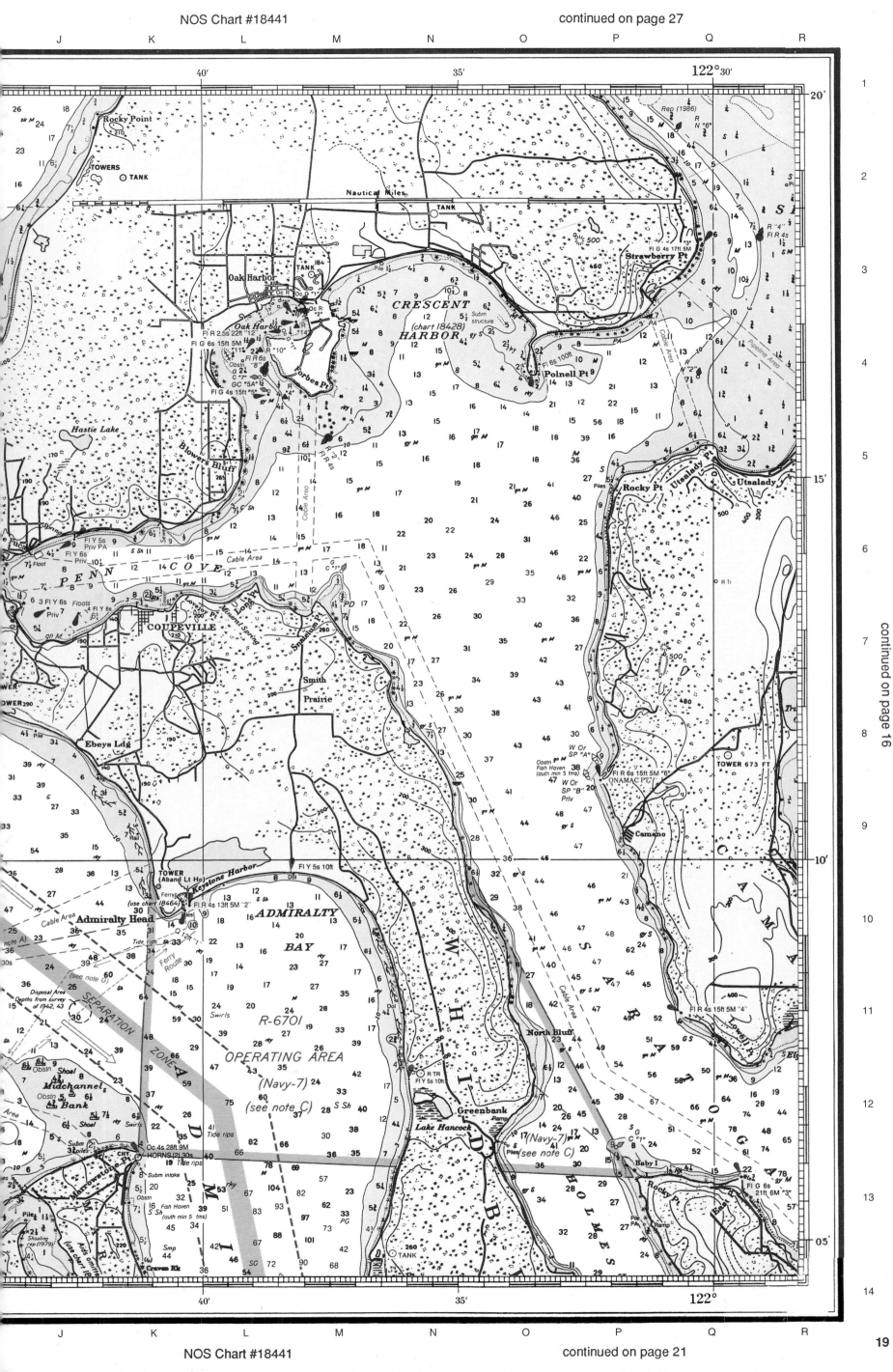

continued on page 21

continued on page 16

continued on page 18

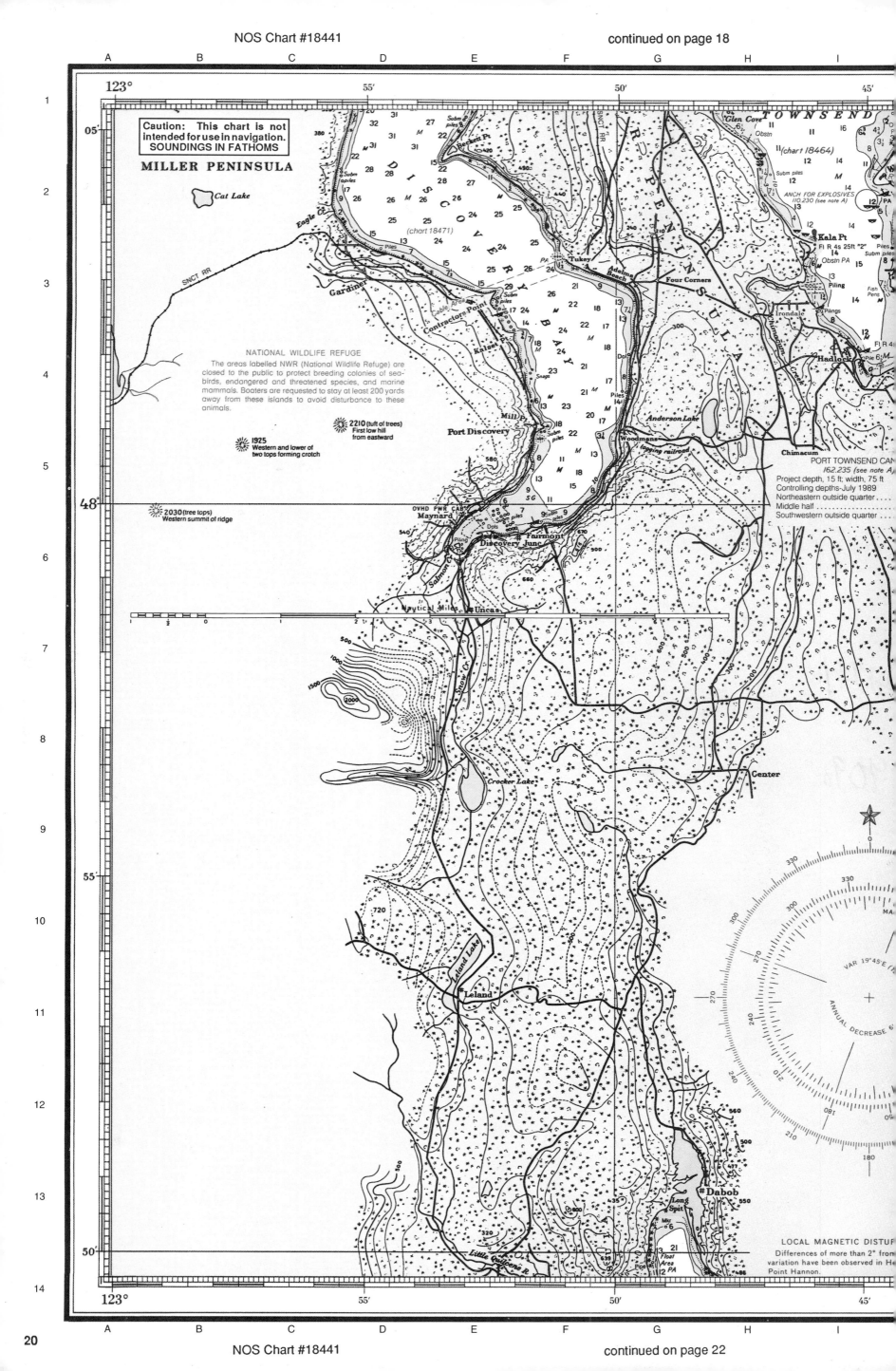

Caution: This chart is not intended for use in navigation. SOUNDINGS IN FATHOMS

MILLER PENINSULA

Cat Lake

DISCOVERY BAY

(chart 18471)

TOWNSEND

(chart 18464)

NATIONAL WILDLIFE REFUGE
The areas labelled NWR (National Wildlife Refuge) are closed to the public to protect breeding colonies of seabirds, endangered and threatened species, and marine mammals. Boaters are requested to stay at least 200 yards away from these islands to avoid disturbance to these animals.

2210 (tuft of trees) First low hill from eastward

1925 Western and lower of two tops forming crotch

2030 (tree tops) Western summit of ridge

Port Discovery

PORT TOWNSEND CAN
162.235 (see note A)
Project depth, 15 ft; width, 75 ft
Controlling depths-July 1989
Northeastern outside quarter . . . .
Middle half . . . .
Southwestern outside quarter . . .

Nautical Miles

LOCAL MAGNETIC DISTUR
Differences of more than 2° in variation have been observed in He
Point Hannon.

continued on page 22

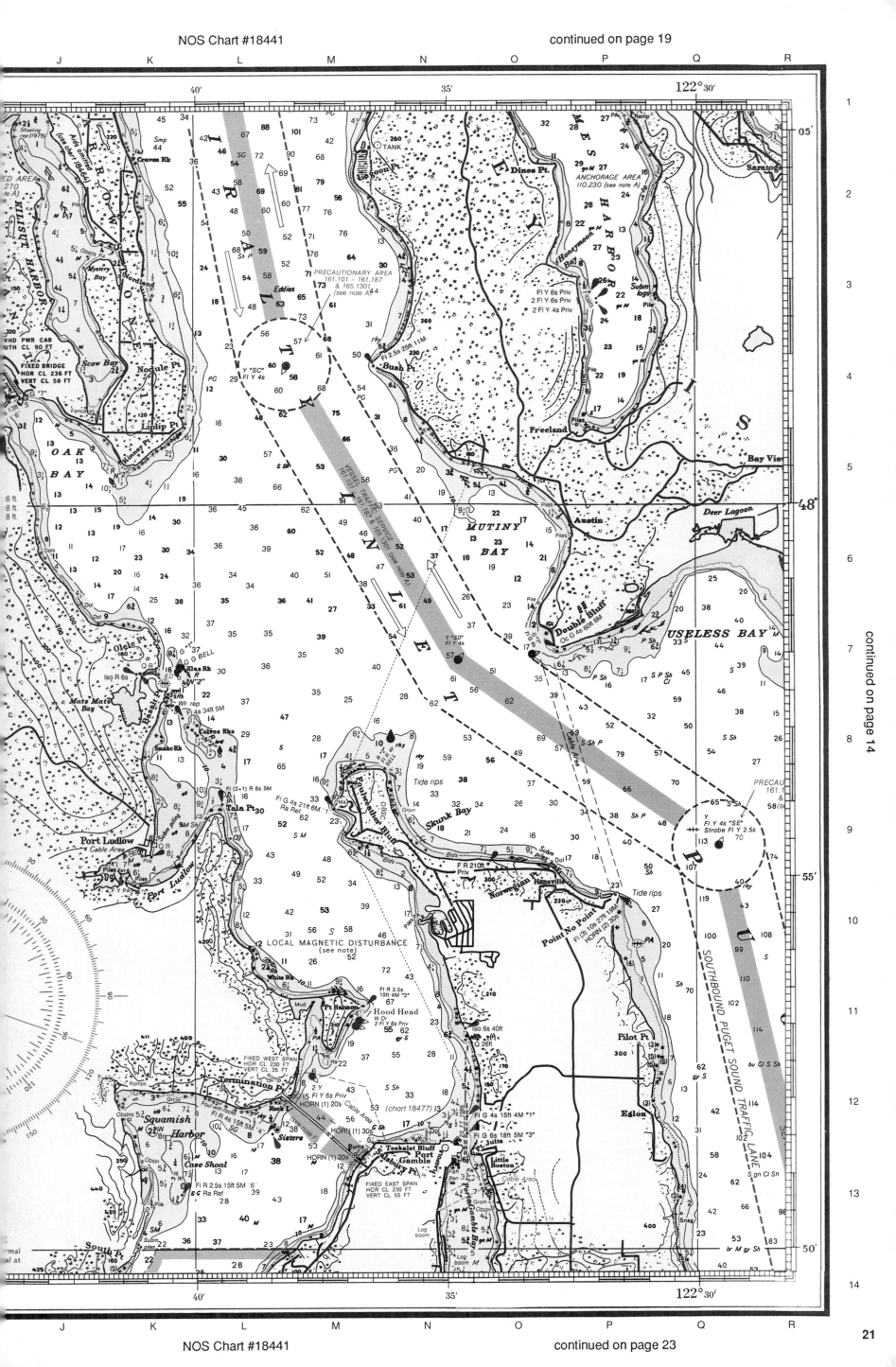

continued on page 14

continued on page 20

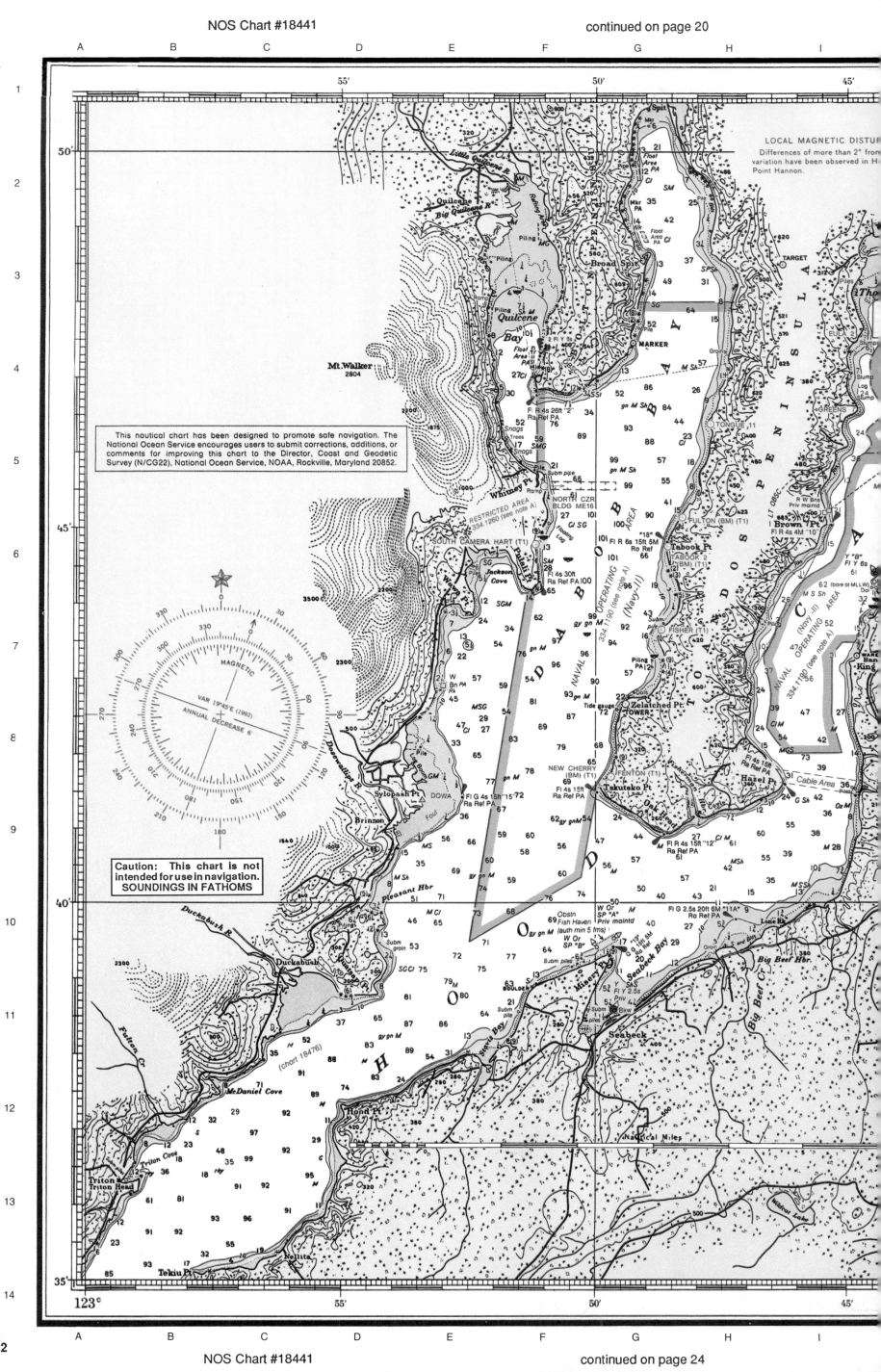

This nautical chart has been designed to promote safe navigation. The National Ocean Service encourages users to submit corrections, additions, or comments for improving this chart to the Director, Coast and Geodetic Survey (N/CG22), National Ocean Service, NOAA, Rockville, Maryland 20852.

Caution: This chart is not intended for use in navigation. SOUNDINGS IN FATHOMS

continued on page 24

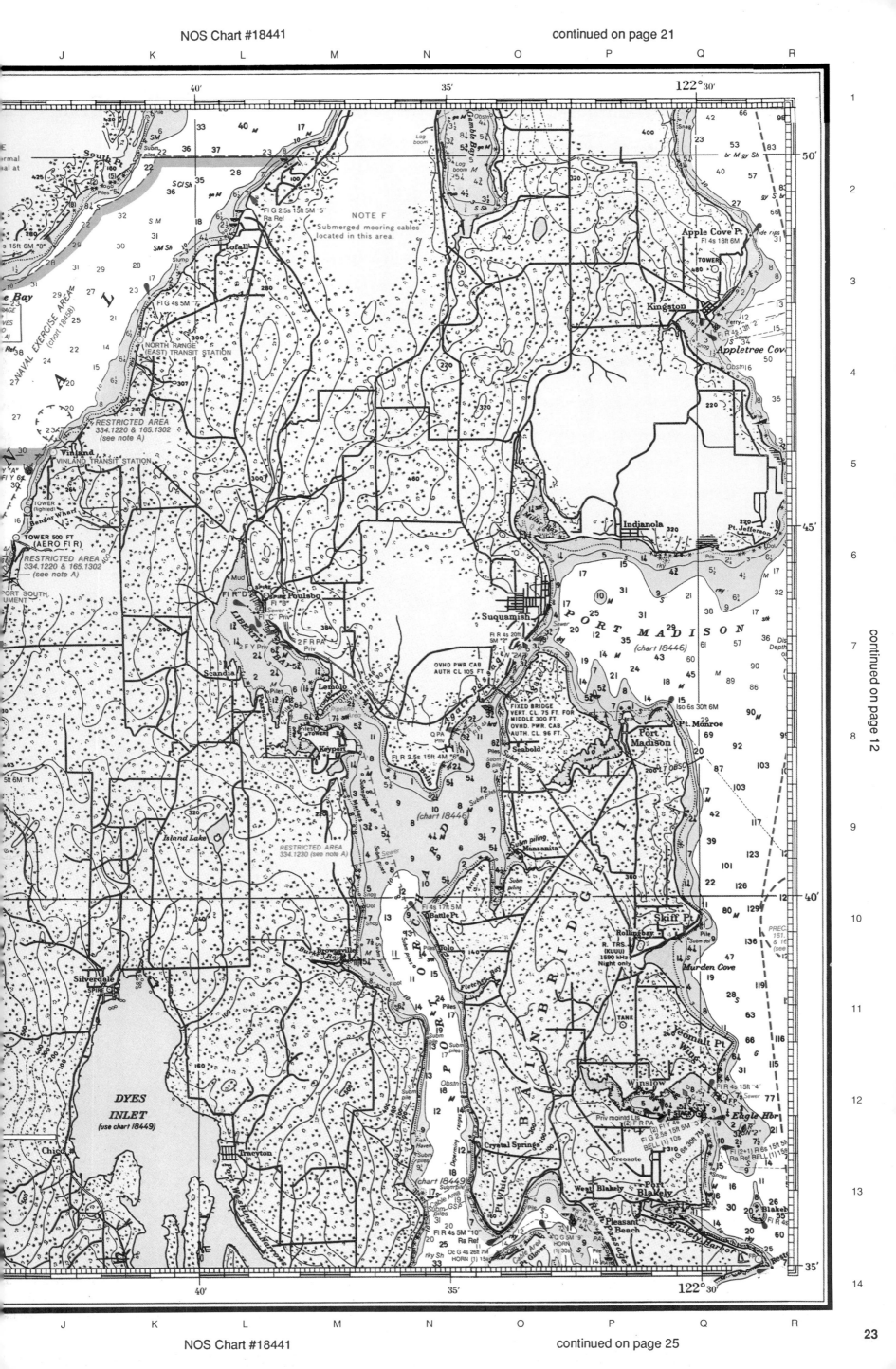

continued on page 12

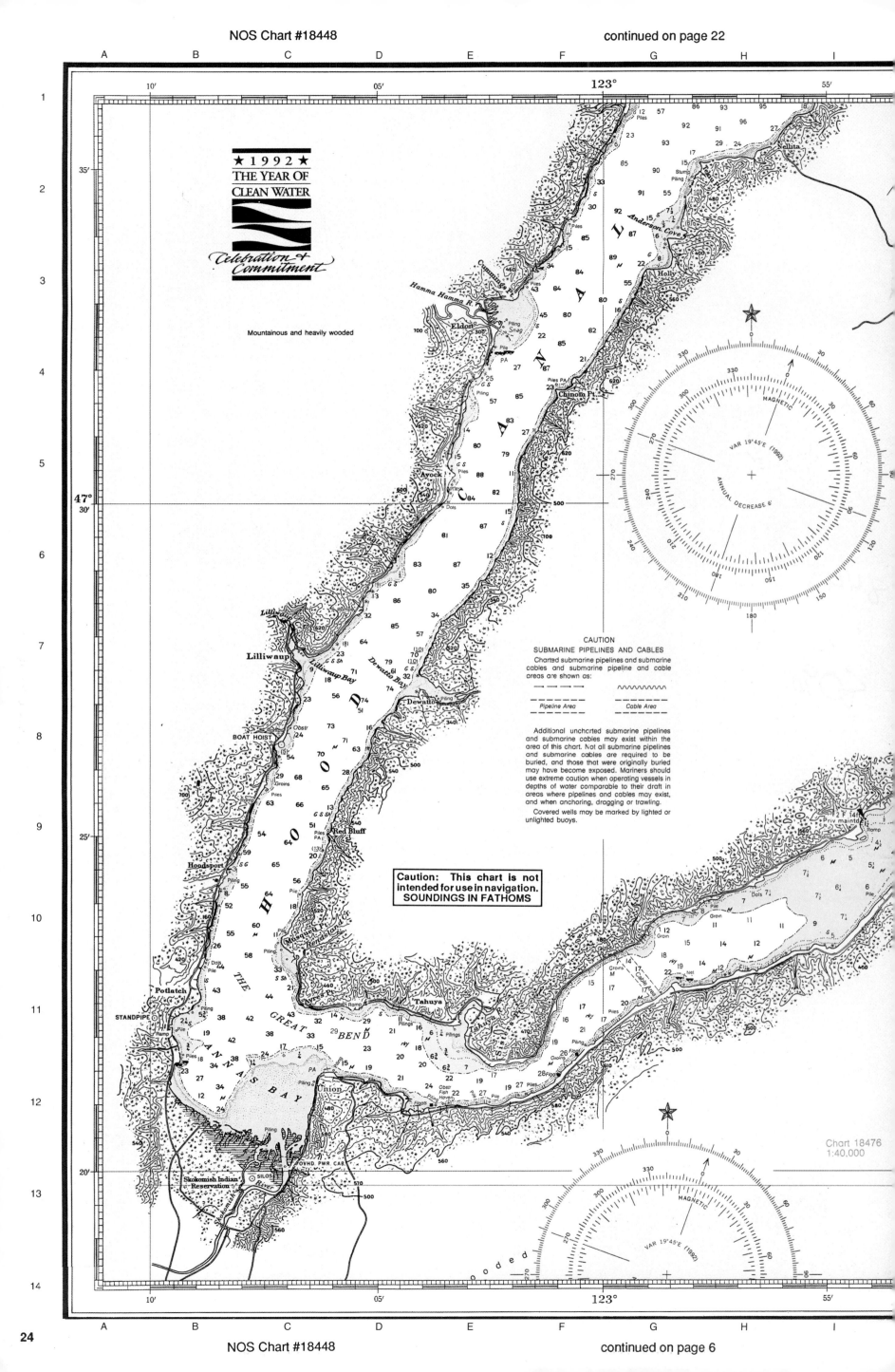

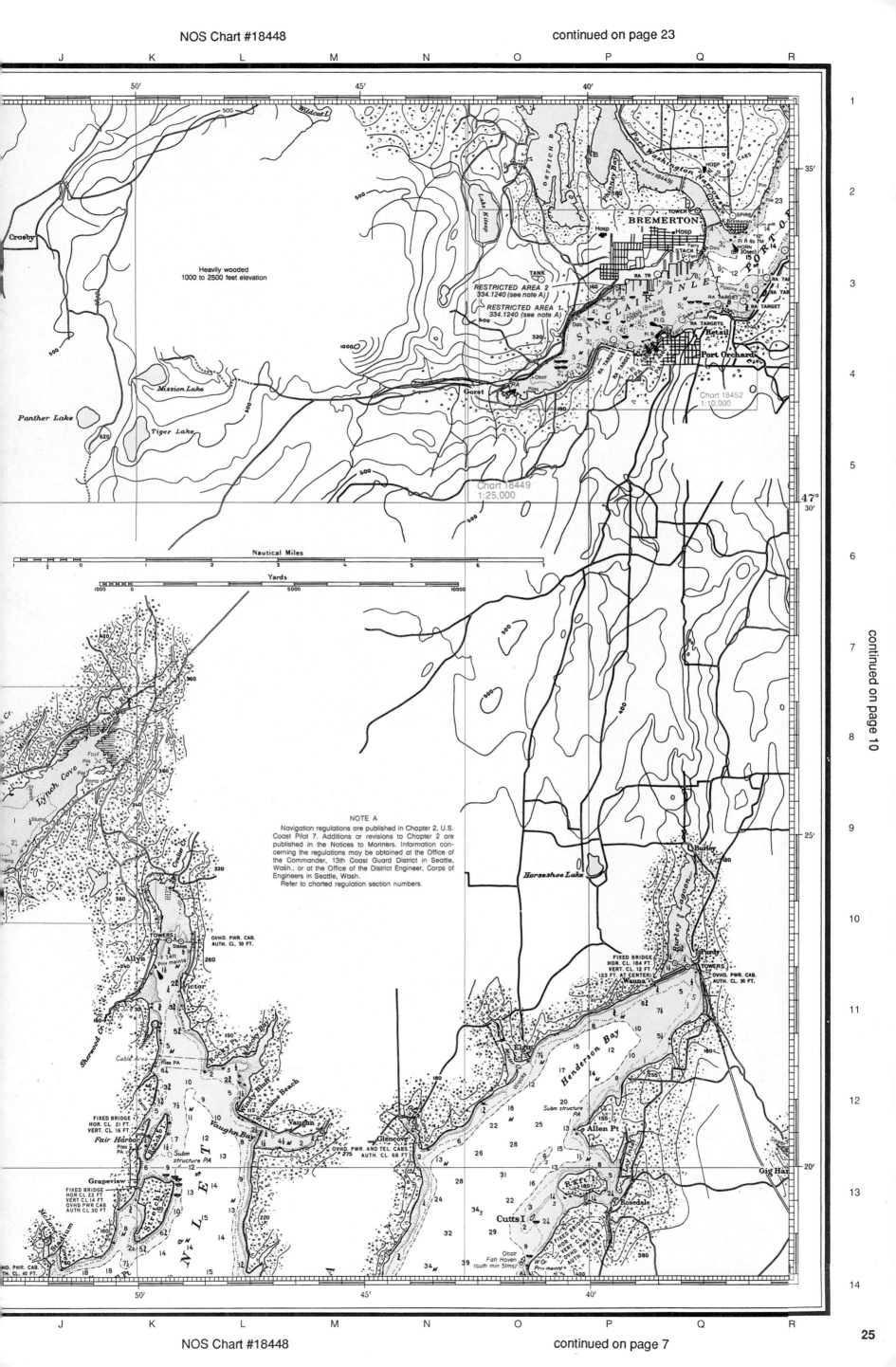

NOTE A

Navigation regulations are published in Chapter 2, U.S. Coast Pilot 7. Additions or revisions to Chapter 2 are published in the Notices to Mariners. Information concerning the regulations may be obtained at the Office of the Commander, 13th Coast Guard District in Seattle, Wash., or at the Office of the District Engineer, Corps of Engineers in Seattle, Wash.
    Refer to charted regulation section numbers.

continued on page 10

continued on page 28

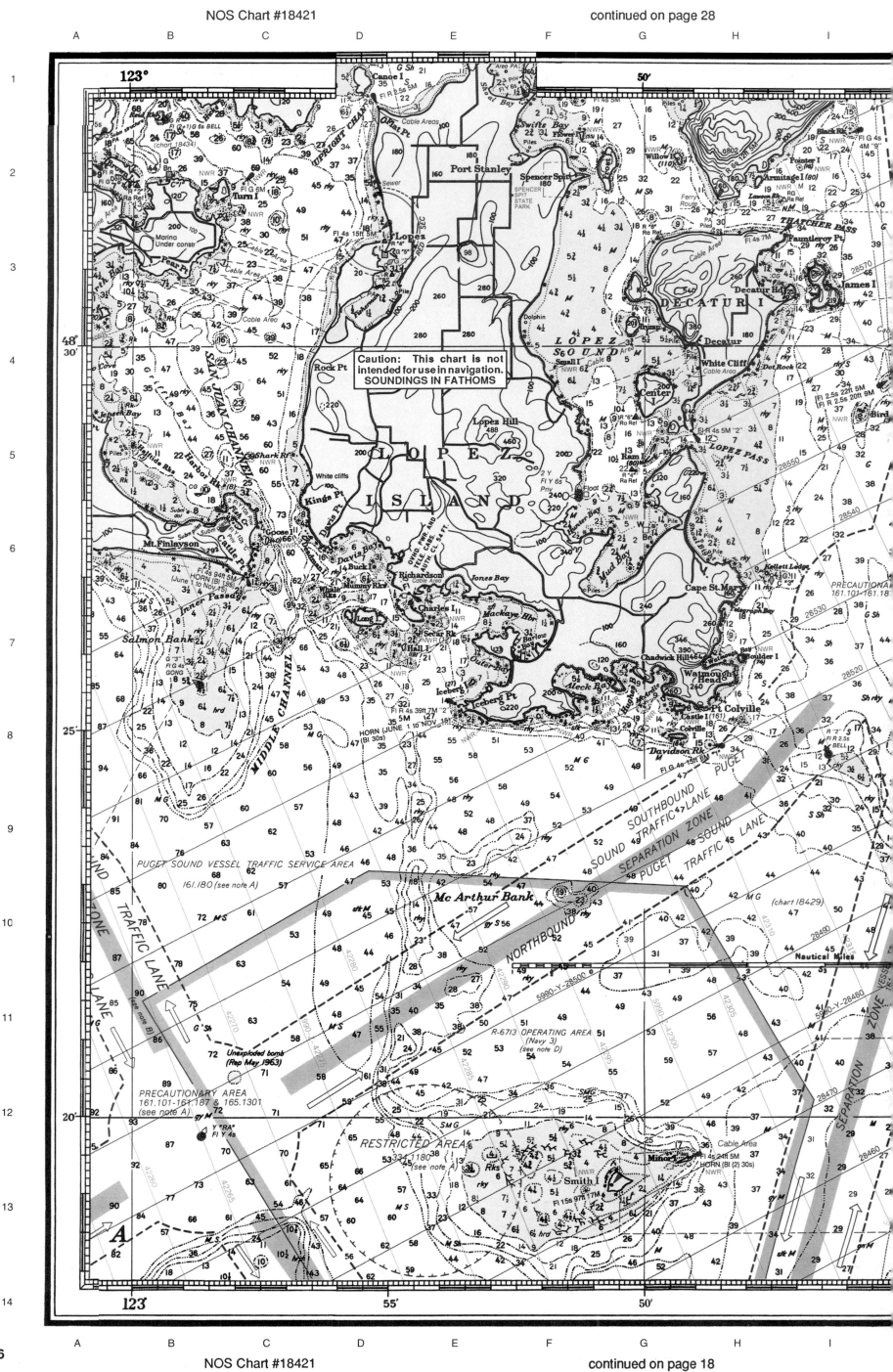

Caution: This chart is not intended for use in navigation.
SOUNDINGS IN FATHOMS

continued on page 18
continued on page 37

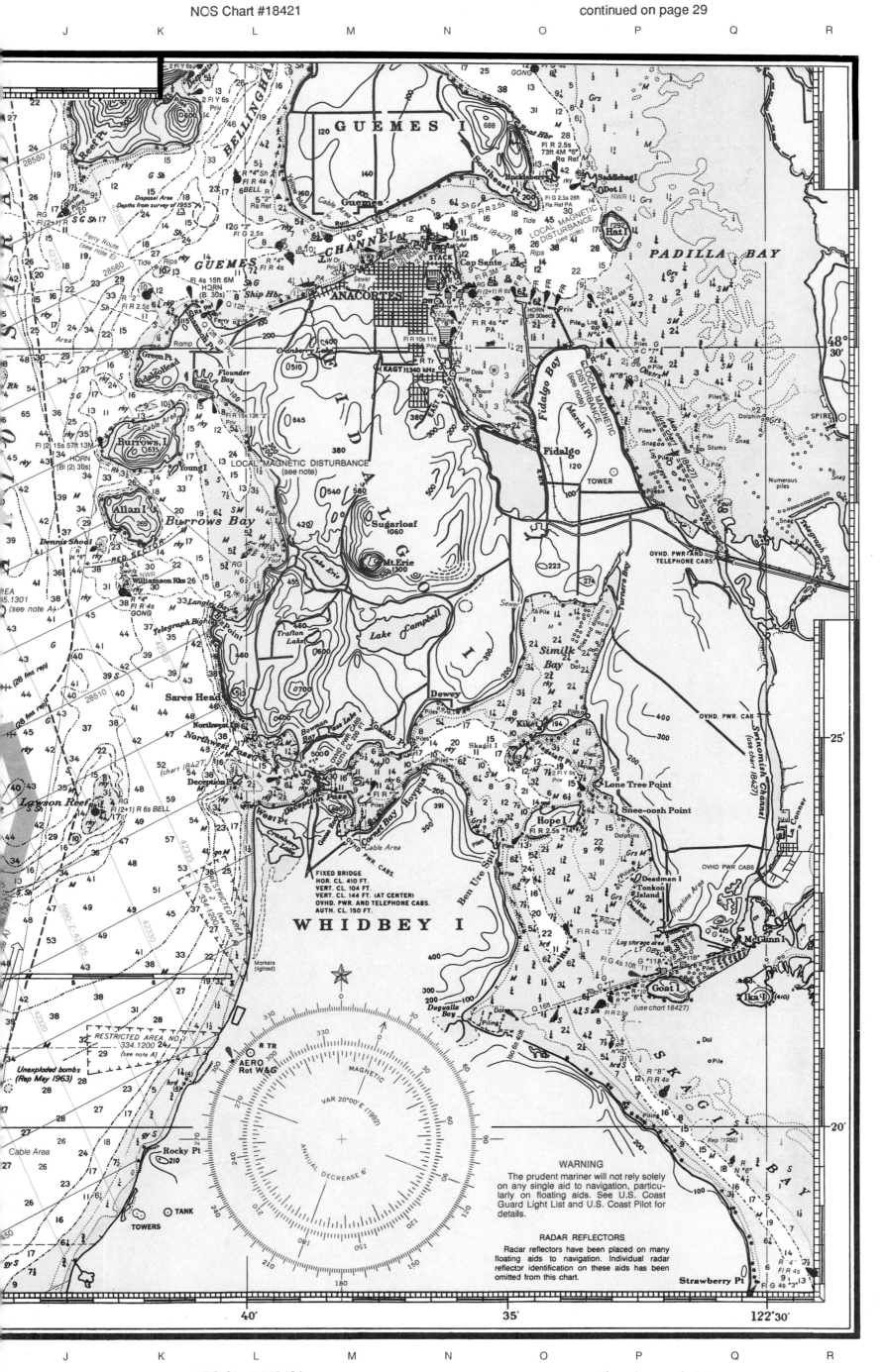

FIXED BRIDGE
HOR. CL. 410 FT.
VERT. CL. 104 FT.
VERT. CL. 144 FT. (AT CENTER)
OVHD. PWR. AND TELEPHONE CABS.
AUTH. CL. 150 FT.

WHIDBEY I

RESTRICTED AREA NO. 1
334.1200 24
(see note A)

Unexploded bombs
(Rep May 1963)

WARNING
The prudent mariner will not rely solely
on any single aid to navigation, particularly on floating aids. See U.S. Coast
Guard Light List and U.S. Coast Pilot for
details.

RADAR REFLECTORS
Radar reflectors have been placed on many
floating aids to navigation. Individual radar
reflector identification on these aids has been
omitted from this chart.

continued on page 30

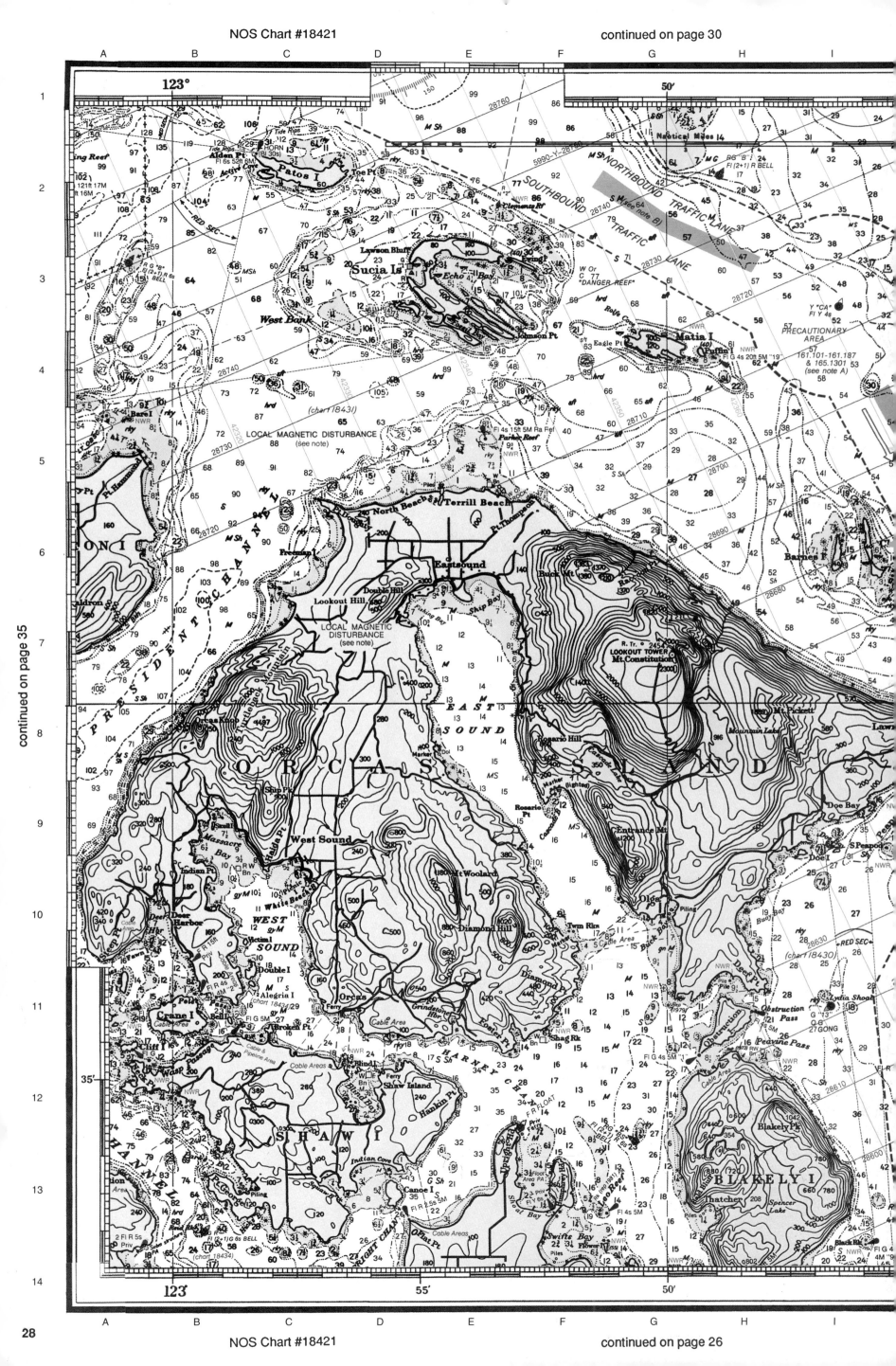

continued on page 35

continued on page 26

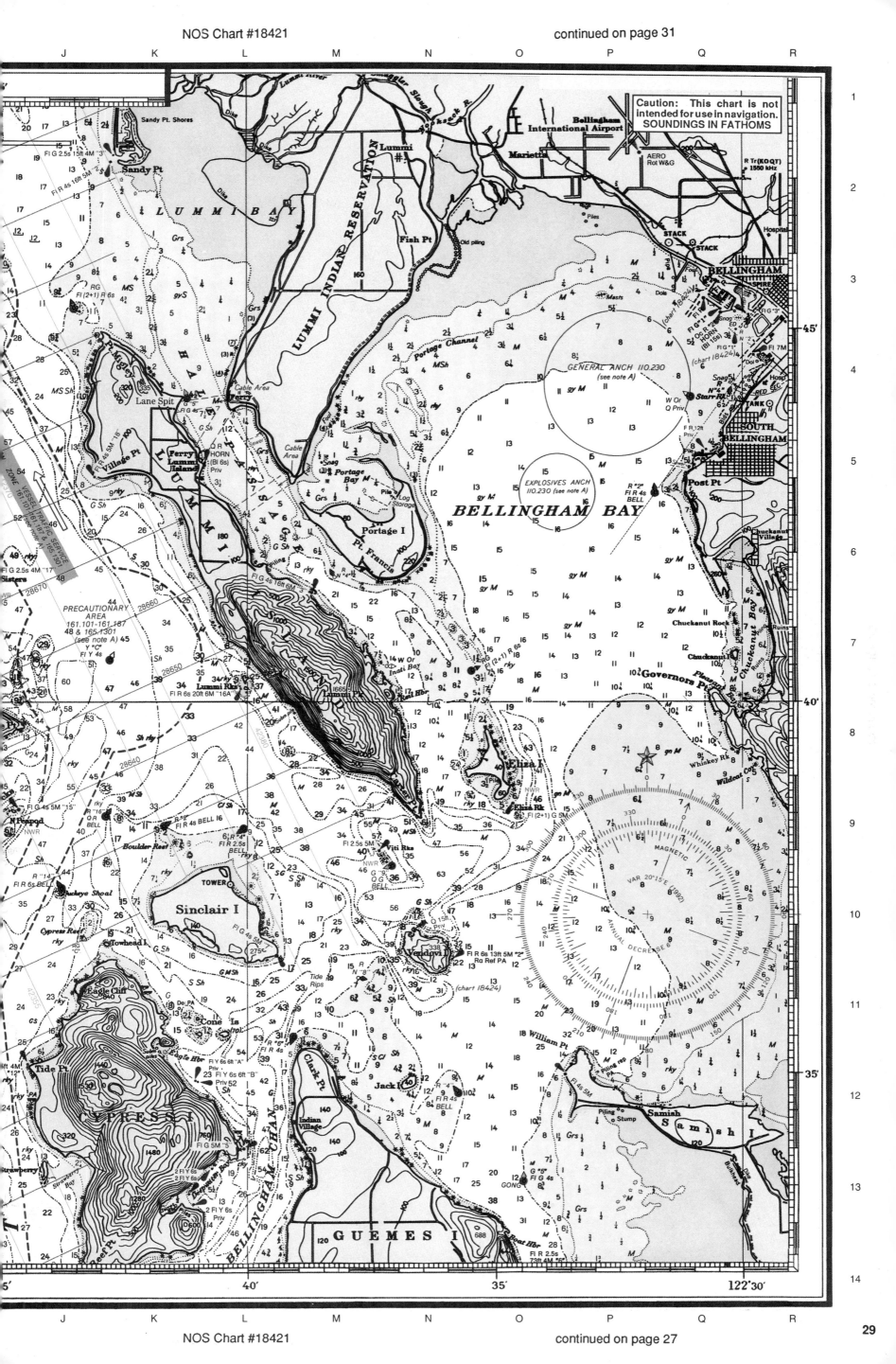

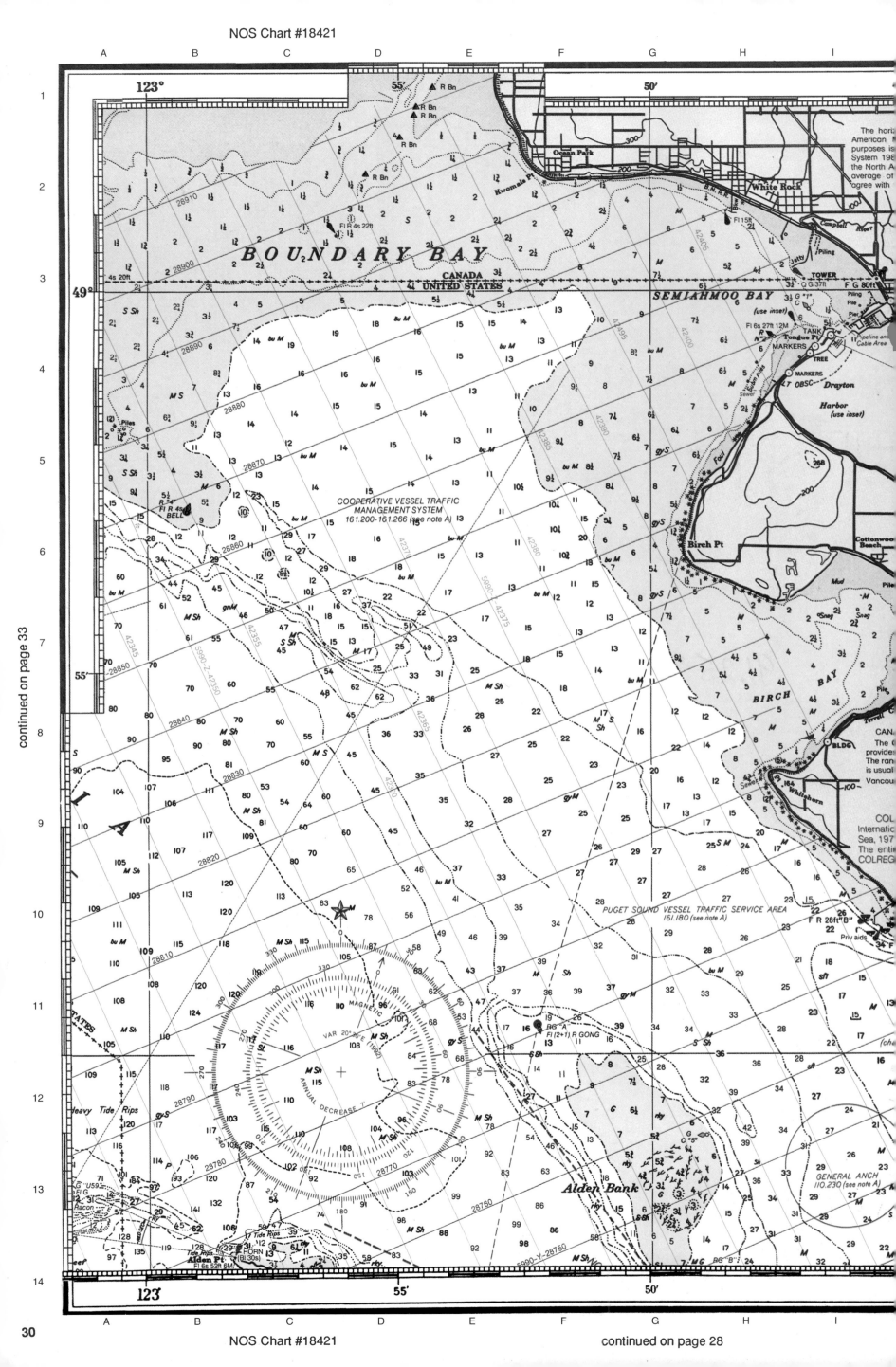

BOUNDARY BAY

CANADA
UNITED STATES

SEMIAHMOO BAY

COOPERATIVE VESSEL TRAFFIC
MANAGEMENT SYSTEM
161.200-161.266 (see note A)

PUGET SOUND VESSEL TRAFFIC SERVICE AREA
161.180 (see note A)

BIRCH BAY

Birch Pt

Drayton
Harbor
(use inset)

Alden Bank

GENERAL ANCH
110.230 (see note A)

Alden Pt
Fl 6s 52ft 6M

Heavy Tide Rips

VAR 20° 0′ E (1992)
ANNUAL DECREASE 7′

continued on page 33

continued on page 28

DRAYTON HARBOR

Mercator Projection
Scale 1:30,000 at Lat. 48°59′

NOTE B
TRAFFIC SEPARATION SERVICE

One-way traffic lanes overprinted on this chart are RECOMMENDED for use by all vessels traveling between the points involved. They have been designed to aid in the prevention of collisions in the Strait of Juan De Fuca and Strait of Georgia waters, but are not intended in any way to supercede or to alter the applicable Rules of the Road. Separation zones are intended to separate inbound and outbound traffic and to be free of ship traffic. Separation zones should not be used except for crossing purposes. When crossing traffic lanes and separation zones use extreme caution.

For information governing the VESSEL TRAFFIC MANAGEMENT AND INFORMATION SYSTEM for the coastal waters of southern British Columbia see Defense Mapping Agency Hydrographic/Topographic Center Publication 154, Sailing Directions (enroute) for British Columbia, and the Sailing Directions, British Columbia Coast (South Portion) Volume 1, published by the Canadian Hydrographic Service.

CAUTION
Improved channels shown by broken lines are subject to shoaling, particularly at the edges.

CAUTION
Temporary changes or defects in aids to navigation are not indicated on this chart. See Notice to Mariners.

NOTE C

For Canadian Firing Practice and Exercise Areas see Canadian Notice to Mariners No. 35 of each year.

NOTE D
NAVAL OPERATING AREAS

Mariners should use caution as naval craft may be maneuvering within the areas. For further information consult Local Notices to Mariners.

LOCAL MAGNETIC DISTURBANCE

Magnetic disturbances exist within the area of this chart. Differences from the normal variation have been observed as follows:

Bellevue Point in Haro Strait	4°
Vicinity of Point Doughty	more than 2°
NW head of East Sound	2°
SE point of Guemes Island	14°
Eastern shore of Burrows Bay	4°
March Point	2°

POLLUTION REPORTS

Report all spills of oil and hazardous substances to the National Response Center via 800-424-8802 (toll free), or to the nearest U.S. Coast Guard facility if telephone communication is impossible (33 CFR 153).

Caution: This chart is not intended for use in navigation.
SOUNDINGS IN FATHOMS

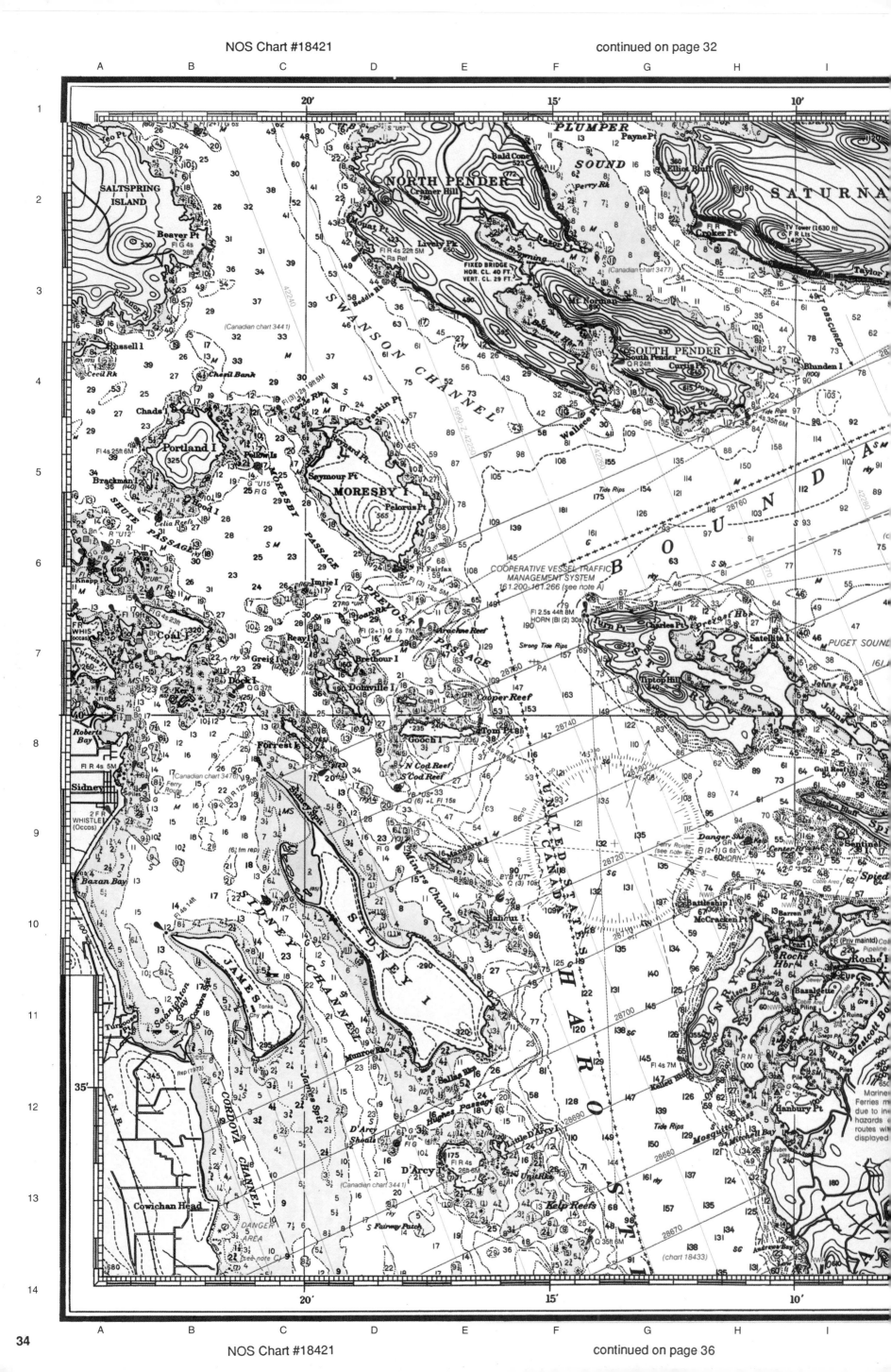

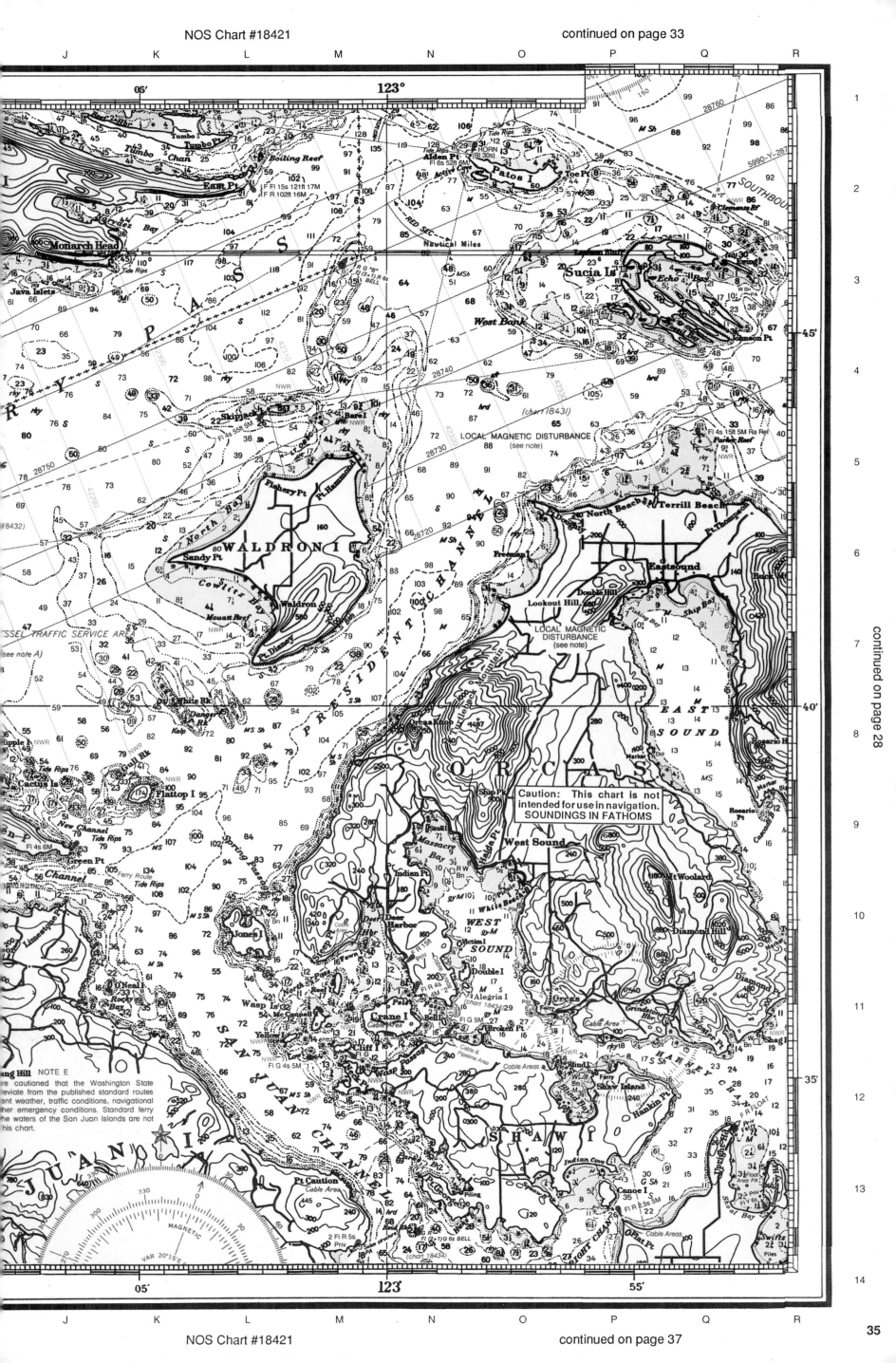

continued on page 28

Caution: This chart is not intended for use in navigation. SOUNDINGS IN FATHOMS

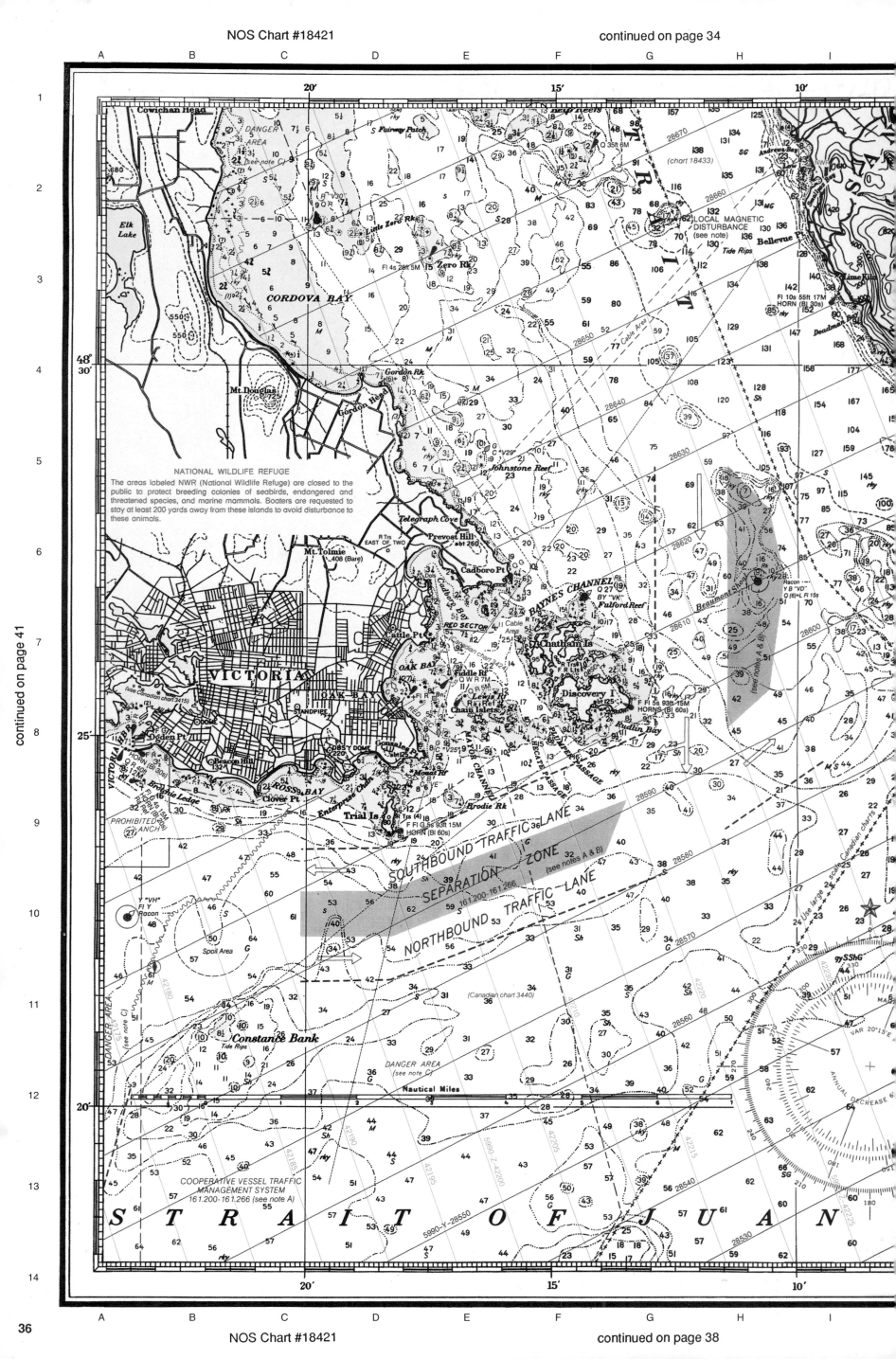

continued on page 41

NATIONAL WILDLIFE REFUGE

The areas labeled NWR (National Wildlife Refuge) are closed to the public to protect breeding colonies of seabirds, endangered and threatened species, and marine mammals. Boaters are requested to stay at least 200 yards away from these islands to avoid disturbance to these animals.

LOCAL MAGNETIC DISTURBANCE (see note)

COOPERATIVE VESSEL TRAFFIC MANAGEMENT SYSTEM 161.200-161.266 (see note A)

S T R A I T   O F   J U A N

SOUTHBOUND TRAFFIC LANE

SEPARATION ZONE (see notes A & B)

NORTHBOUND TRAFFIC LANE

CORDOVA BAY

VICTORIA

OAK BAY

Constance Bank

continued on page 35

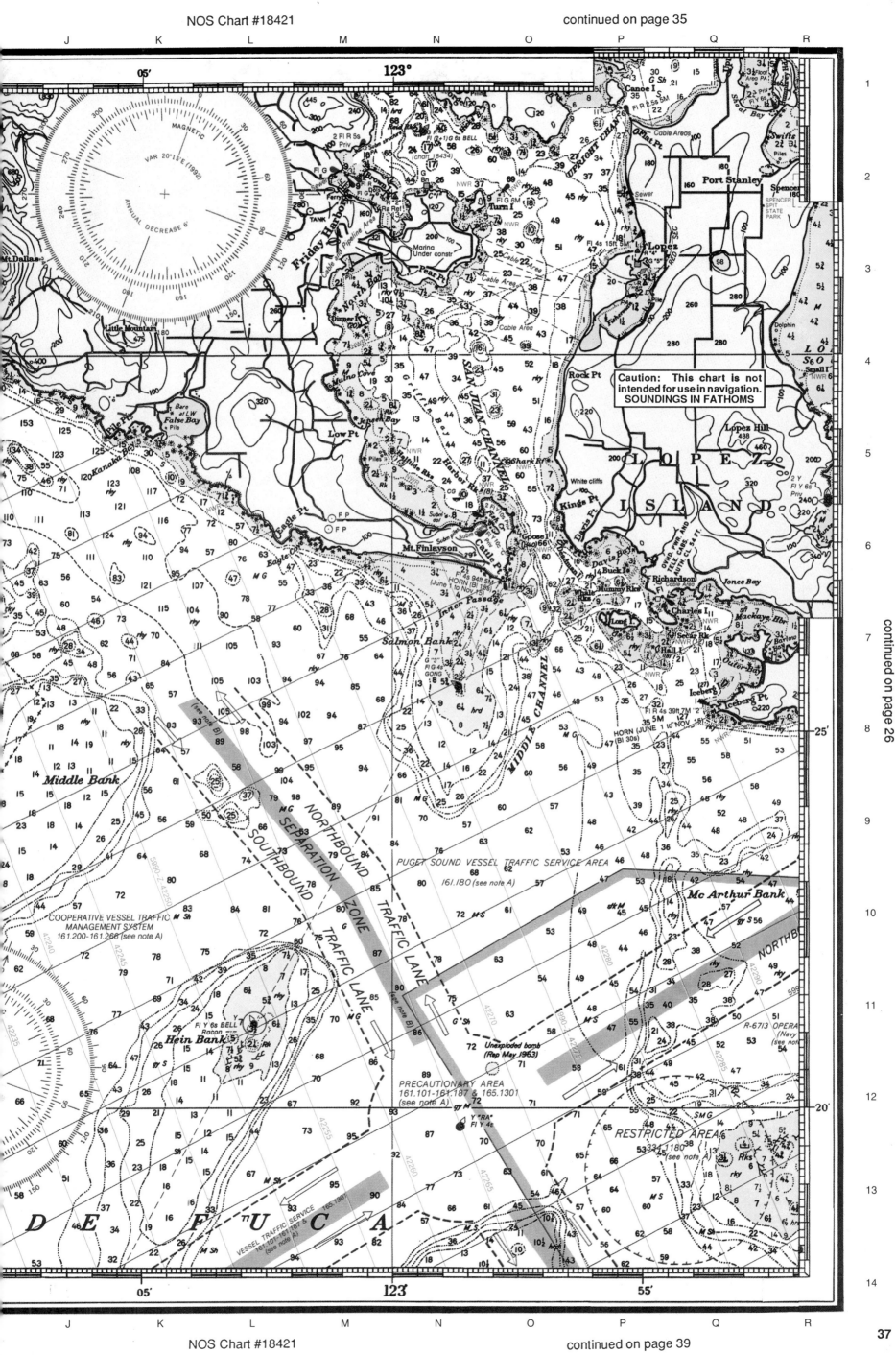

Caution: This chart is not intended for use in navigation. SOUNDINGS IN FATHOMS

continued on page 26

continued on page 39

continued on page 41

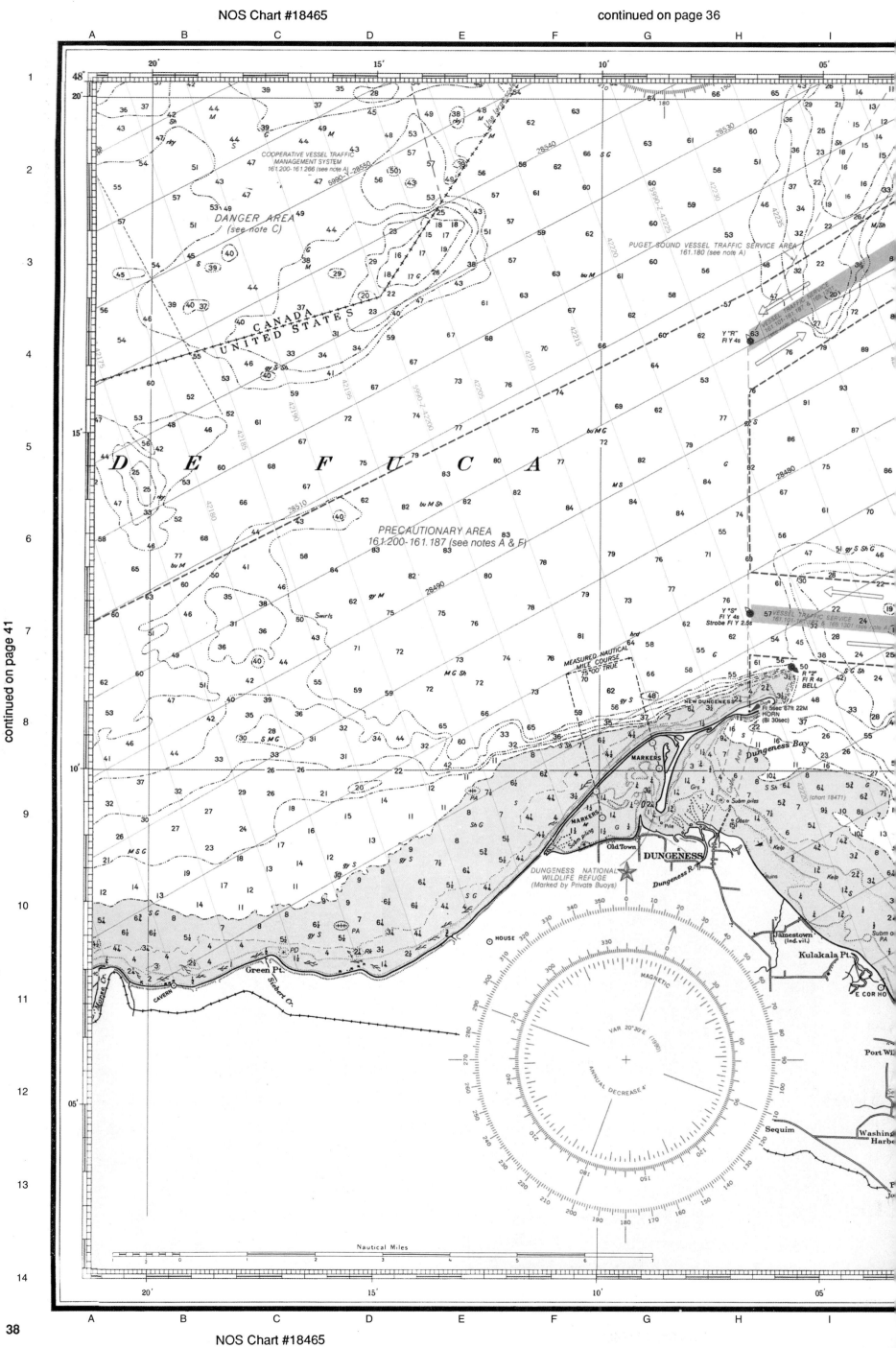

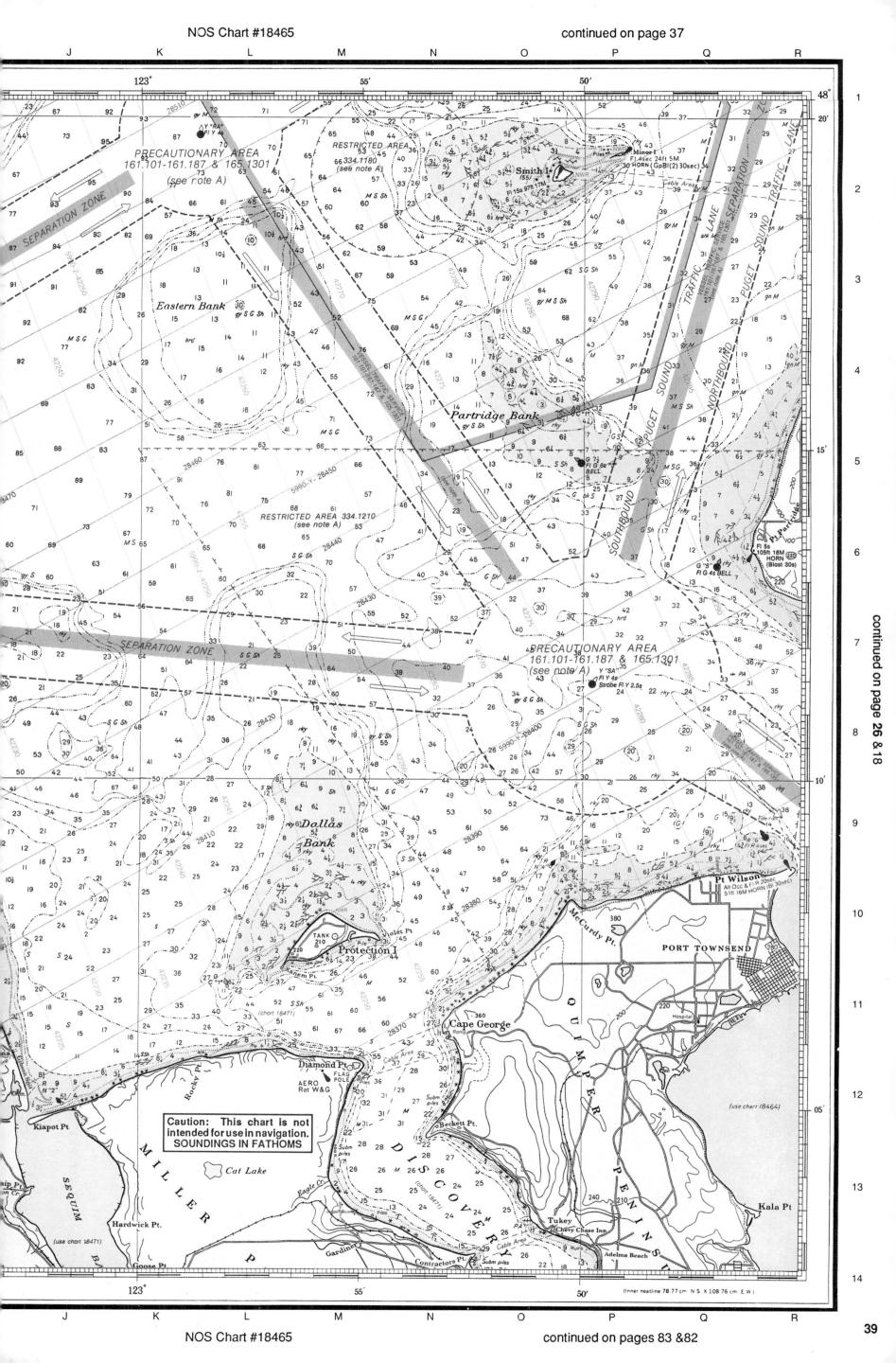

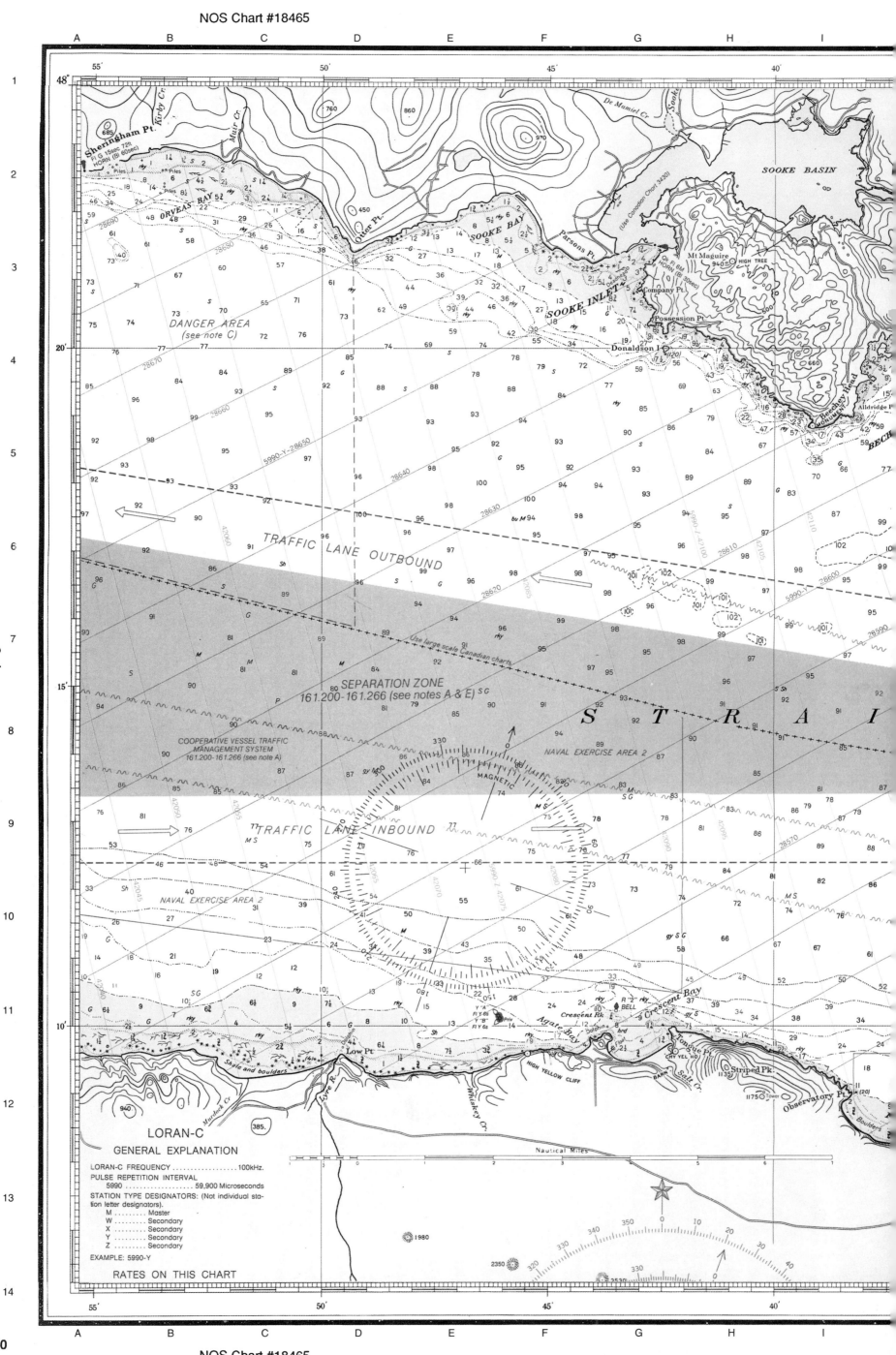

continued on page 43

LORAN-C

GENERAL EXPLANATION

LORAN-C FREQUENCY .... 100kHz.
PULSE REPETITION INTERVAL
5990 .... 59,900 Microseconds.
STATION TYPE DESIGNATORS: (Not individual station letter designators).
M .... Master
W .... Secondary
X .... Secondary
Y .... Secondary
Z .... Secondary
EXAMPLE: 5990-Y

RATES ON THIS CHART

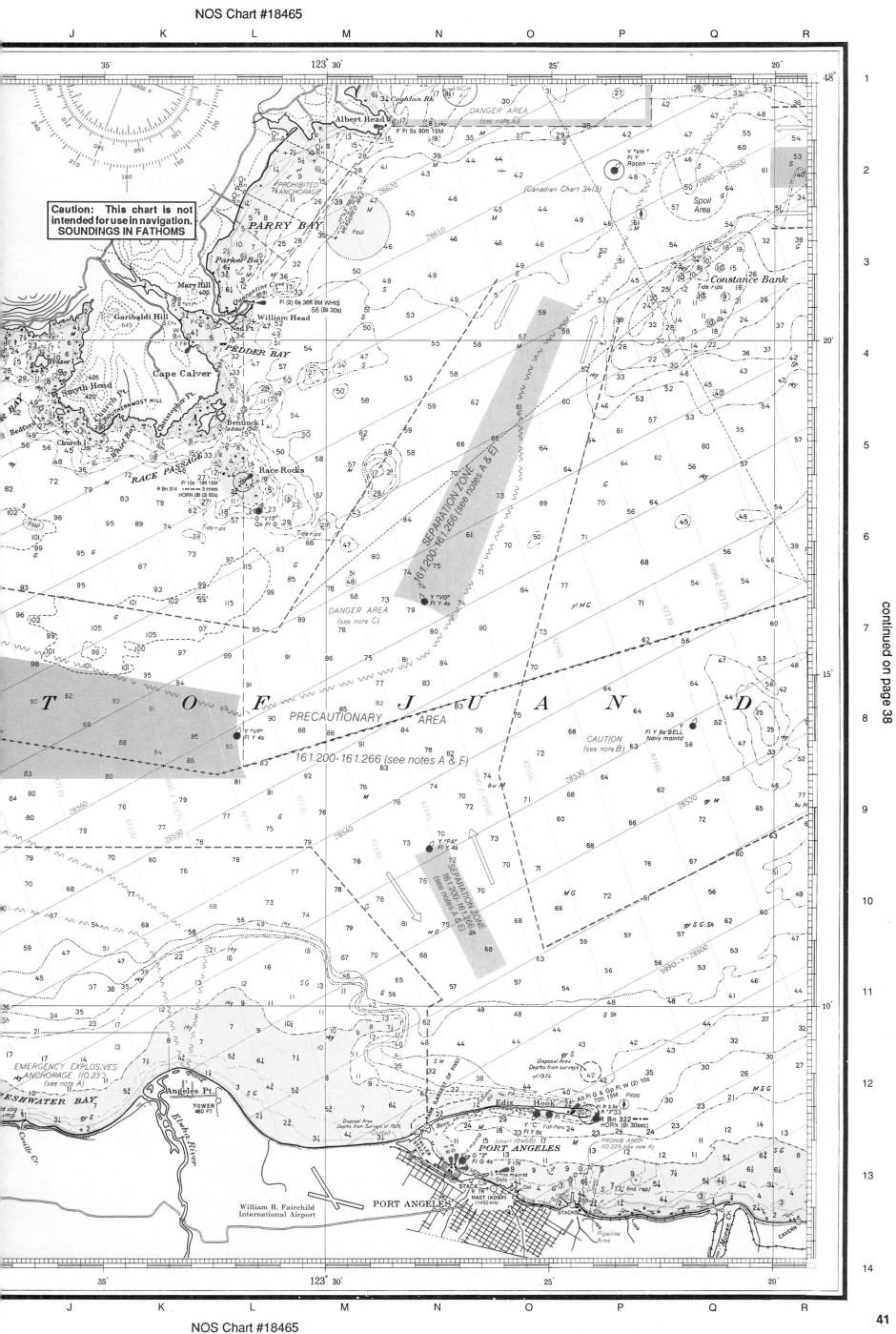

continued on page 38

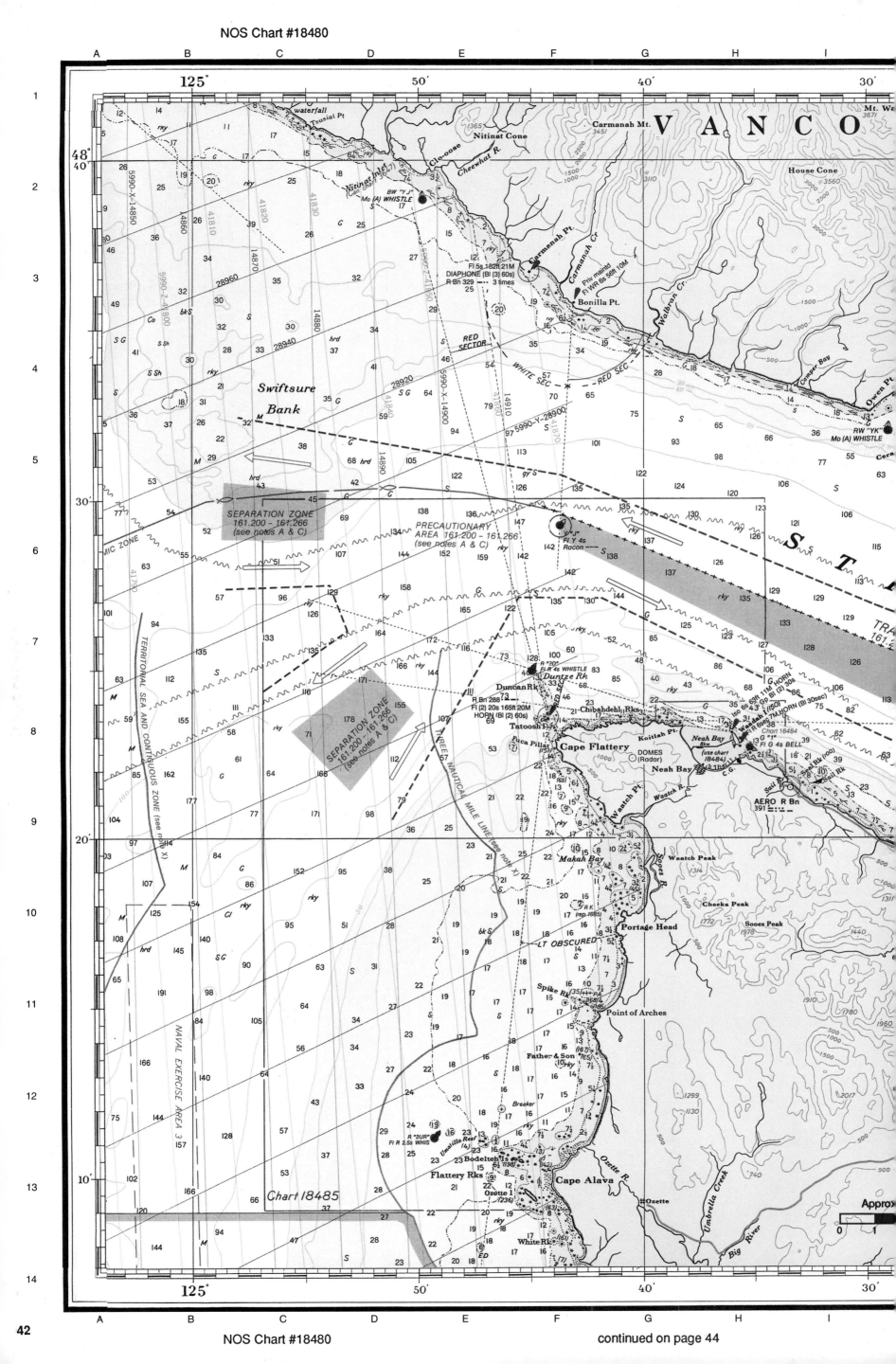

continued on page 44

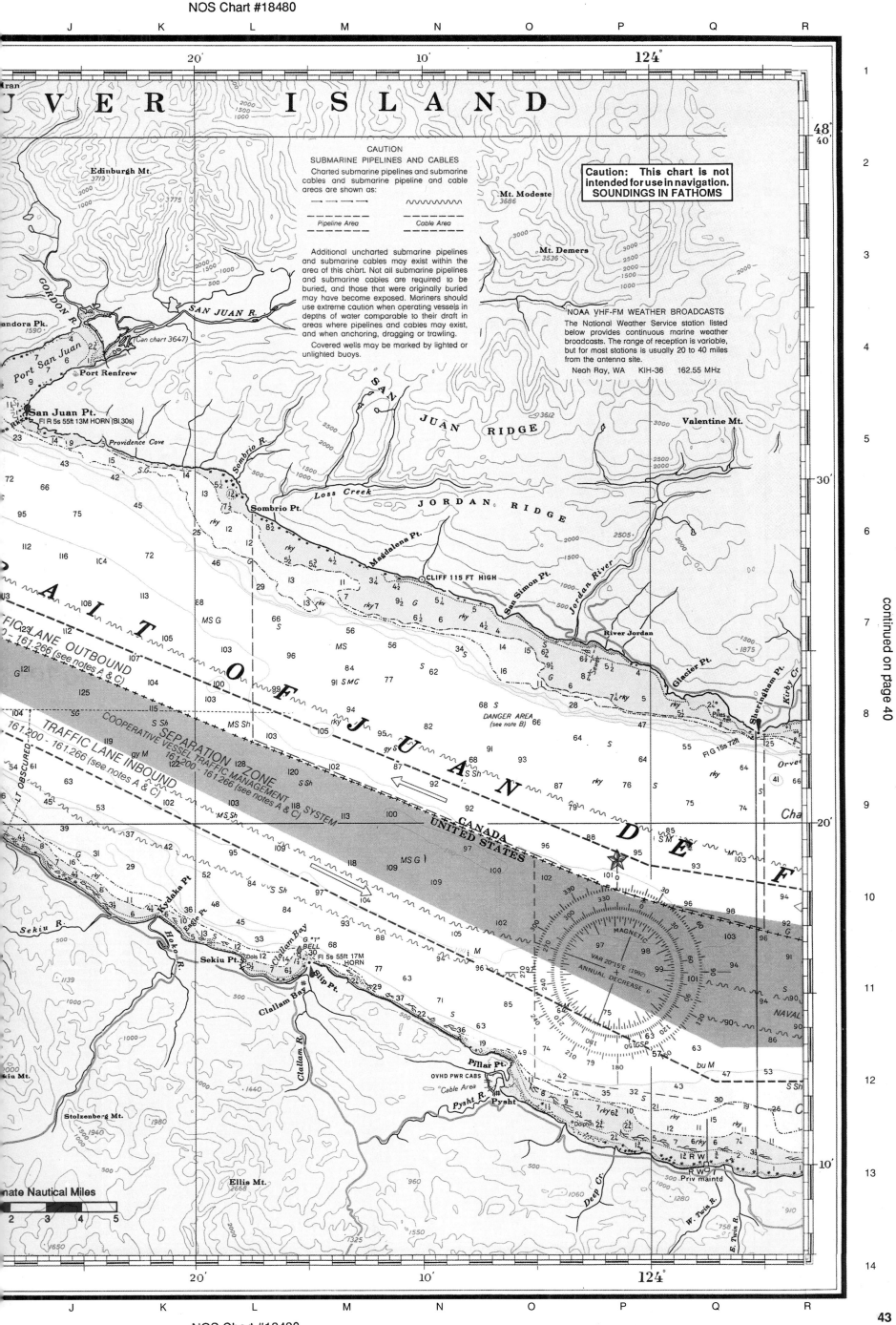

continued on page 40

CAUTION
SUBMARINE PIPELINES AND CABLES
Charted submarine pipelines and submarine cables and submarine pipeline and cable areas are shown as:

Pipeline Area   Cable Area

Additional uncharted submarine pipelines and submarine cables may exist within the area of this chart. Not all submarine pipelines and submarine cables are required to be buried, and those that were originally buried may have become exposed. Mariners should use extreme caution when operating vessels in depths of water comparable to their draft in areas where pipelines and cables may exist, and when anchoring, dragging or trawling.

Covered wells may be marked by lighted or unlighted buoys.

Caution: This chart is not intended for use in navigation.
SOUNDINGS IN FATHOMS

NOAA VHF-FM WEATHER BROADCASTS
The National Weather Service station listed below provides continuous marine weather broadcasts. The range of reception is variable, but for most stations is usually 20 to 40 miles from the antenna site.
Neah Bay, WA   KIH-36   162.55 MHz

UVER ISLAND

Edinburgh Mt.

Mt. Modeste

Mt. Demers

SAN JUAN RIDGE

Valentine Mt.

JORDAN RIDGE

STRAIT OF JUAN DE FUCA

TRAFFIC LANE OUTBOUND
161.200 - 161.266 (see notes A & C)

SEPARATION ZONE
COOPERATIVE VESSEL TRAFFIC MANAGEMENT SYSTEM

TRAFFIC LANE INBOUND
161.200 - 161.266 (see notes A & C)

CANADA
UNITED STATES

DANGER AREA
(see note B)

MAGNETIC
VAR 20°15'E (1992)
ANNUAL DECREASE 6'

Sekiu R.
Hoko R.
Sekiu Pt.
Clallam Bay
Slip Pt.
Clallam Bay
Clallam R.

Pillar Pt.
OVHD PWR CABS
Cable Area
Pysht R.   Pysht

Stolzenberg Mt.

Ellis Mt.

Deep Cr.

W. Twin R.

E. Twin R.

nate Nautical Miles

continued on page 44

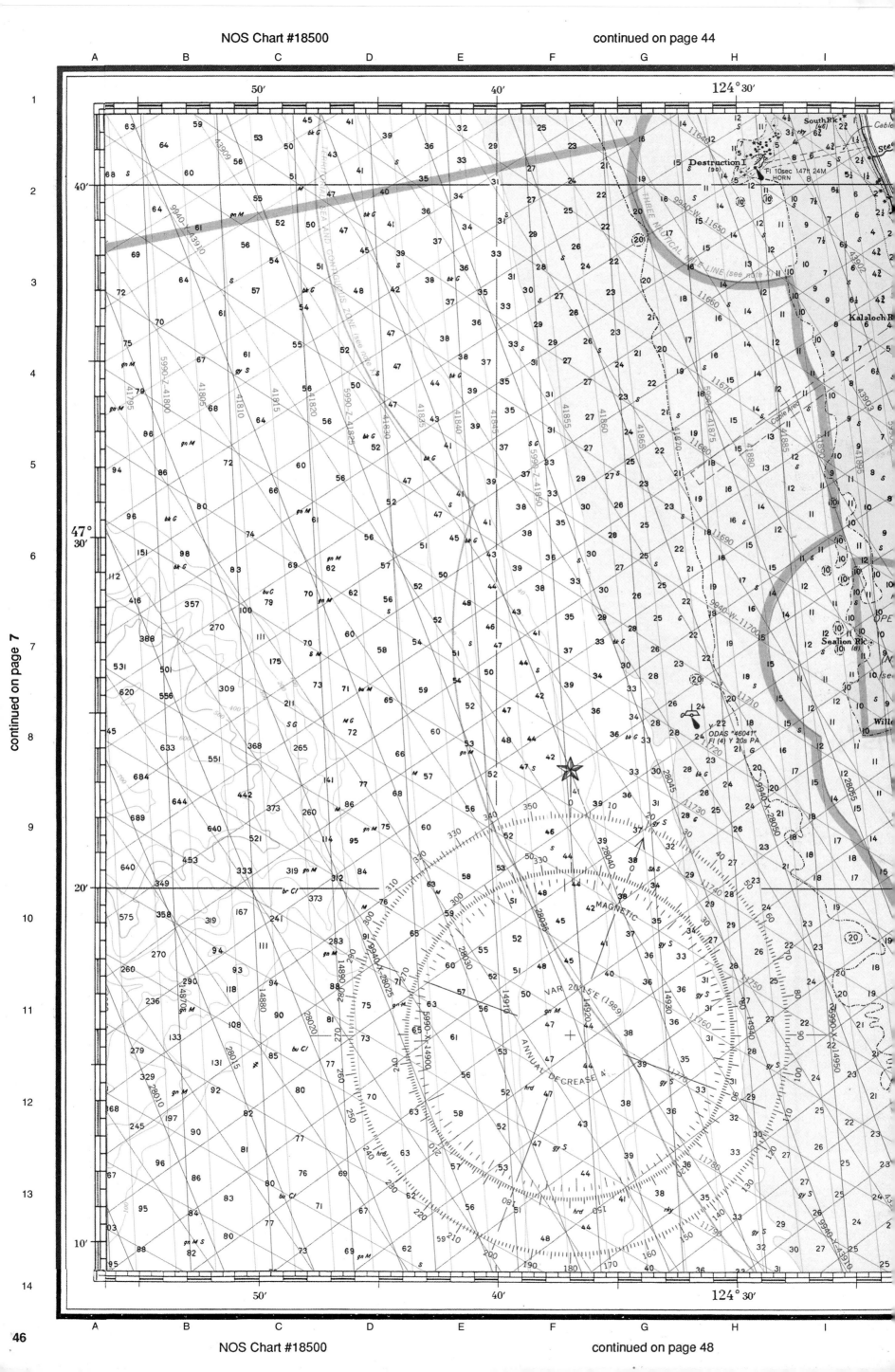

continued on page 7

continued on page 48

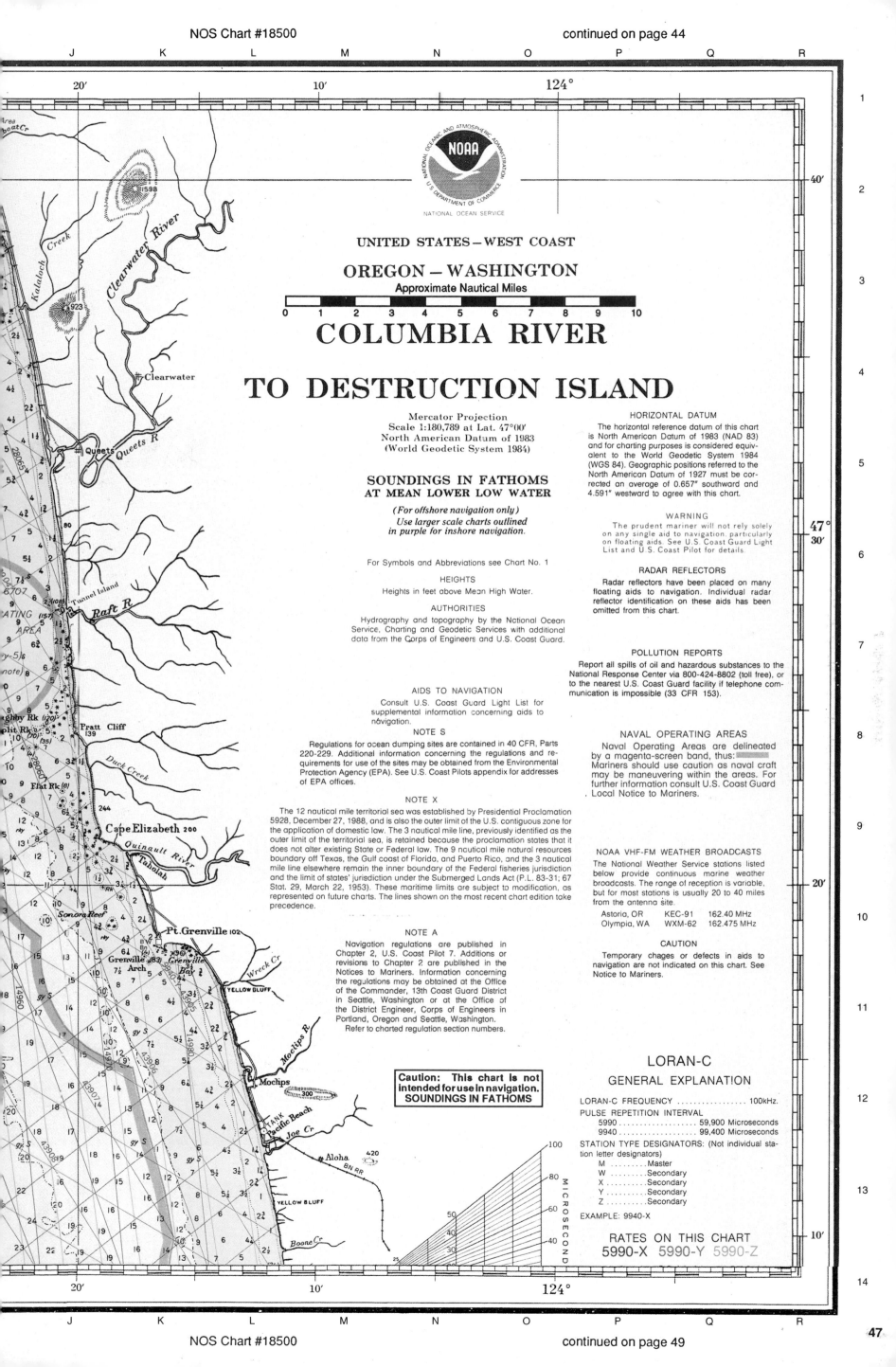

UNITED STATES—WEST COAST

OREGON — WASHINGTON

Approximate Nautical Miles

0 1 2 3 4 5 6 7 8 9 10

COLUMBIA RIVER

TO DESTRUCTION ISLAND

Mercator Projection
Scale 1:180,789 at Lat. 47°00'
North American Datum of 1983
(World Geodetic System 1984)

SOUNDINGS IN FATHOMS
AT MEAN LOWER LOW WATER

(For offshore navigation only)
Use larger scale charts outlined
in purple for inshore navigation.

For Symbols and Abbreviations see Chart No. 1

HEIGHTS
Heights in feet above Mean High Water.

AUTHORITIES
Hydrography and topography by the National Ocean Service, Charting and Geodetic Services with additional data from the Corps of Engineers and U.S. Coast Guard.

AIDS TO NAVIGATION
Consult U.S. Coast Guard Light List for supplemental information concerning aids to navigation.

NOTE S
Regulations for ocean dumping sites are contained in 40 CFR, Parts 220-229. Additional information concerning the regulations and requirements for use of the sites may be obtained from the Environmental Protection Agency (EPA). See U.S. Coast Pilots appendix for addresses of EPA offices.

NOTE X
The 12 nautical mile territorial sea was established by Presidential Proclamation 5928, December 27, 1988, and is also the outer limit of the U.S. contiguous zone for the application of domestic law. The 3 nautical mile line, previously identified as the outer limit of the territorial sea, is retained because the proclamation states that it does not alter existing State or Federal law. The 9 nautical mile natural resources boundary off Texas, the Gulf coast of Florida, and Puerto Rico, and the 3 nautical mile line elsewhere remain the inner boundary of the Federal fisheries jurisdiction and the limit of states' jurisdiction under the Submerged Lands Act (P.L. 83-31; 67 Stat. 29, March 22, 1953). These maritime limits are subject to modification, as represented on future charts. The lines shown on the most recent chart edition take precedence.

NOTE A
Navigation regulations are published in Chapter 2, U.S. Coast Pilot 7. Additions or revisions to Chapter 2 are published in the Notices to Mariners. Information concerning the regulations may be obtained at the Office of the Commander, 13th Coast Guard District in Seattle, Washington or at the Office of the District Engineer, Corps of Engineers in Portland, Oregon and Seattle, Washington.
Refer to charted regulation section numbers.

Caution: This chart is not intended for use in navigation. SOUNDINGS IN FATHOMS

HORIZONTAL DATUM
The horizontal reference datum of this chart is North American Datum of 1983 (NAD 83) and for charting purposes is considered equivalent to the World Geodetic System 1984 (WGS 84). Geographic positions referred to the North American Datum of 1927 must be corrected an average of 0.657″ southward and 4.591″ westward to agree with this chart.

WARNING
The prudent mariner will not rely solely on any single aid to navigation, particularly on floating aids. See U.S. Coast Guard Light List and U.S. Coast Pilot for details.

RADAR REFLECTORS
Radar reflectors have been placed on many floating aids to navigation. Individual radar reflector identification on these aids has been omitted from this chart.

POLLUTION REPORTS
Report all spills of oil and hazardous substances to the National Response Center via 800-424-8802 (toll free), or to the nearest U.S. Coast Guard facility if telephone communication is impossible (33 CFR 153).

NAVAL OPERATING AREAS
Naval Operating Areas are delineated by a magenta-screen band, thus: ▨ Mariners should use caution as naval craft may be maneuvering within the areas. For further information consult U.S. Coast Guard Local Notice to Mariners.

NOAA VHF-FM WEATHER BROADCASTS
The National Weather Service stations listed below provide continuous marine weather broadcasts. The range of reception is variable, but for most stations is usually 20 to 40 miles from the antenna site.

Astoria, OR	KEC-91	162.40 MHz
Olympia, WA	WXM-62	162.475 MHz

CAUTION
Temporary chages or defects in aids to navigation are not indicated on this chart. See Notice to Mariners.

LORAN-C
GENERAL EXPLANATION

LORAN-C FREQUENCY .... 100kHz.
PULSE REPETITION INTERVAL
    5990 .... 59,900 Microseconds
    9940 .... 99,400 Microseconds
STATION TYPE DESIGNATORS: (Not individual station letter designators)
    M .... Master
    W .... Secondary
    X .... Secondary
    Y .... Secondary
    Z .... Secondary

EXAMPLE: 9940-X

RATES ON THIS CHART
5990-X   5990-Y   5990-Z

continued on page 46

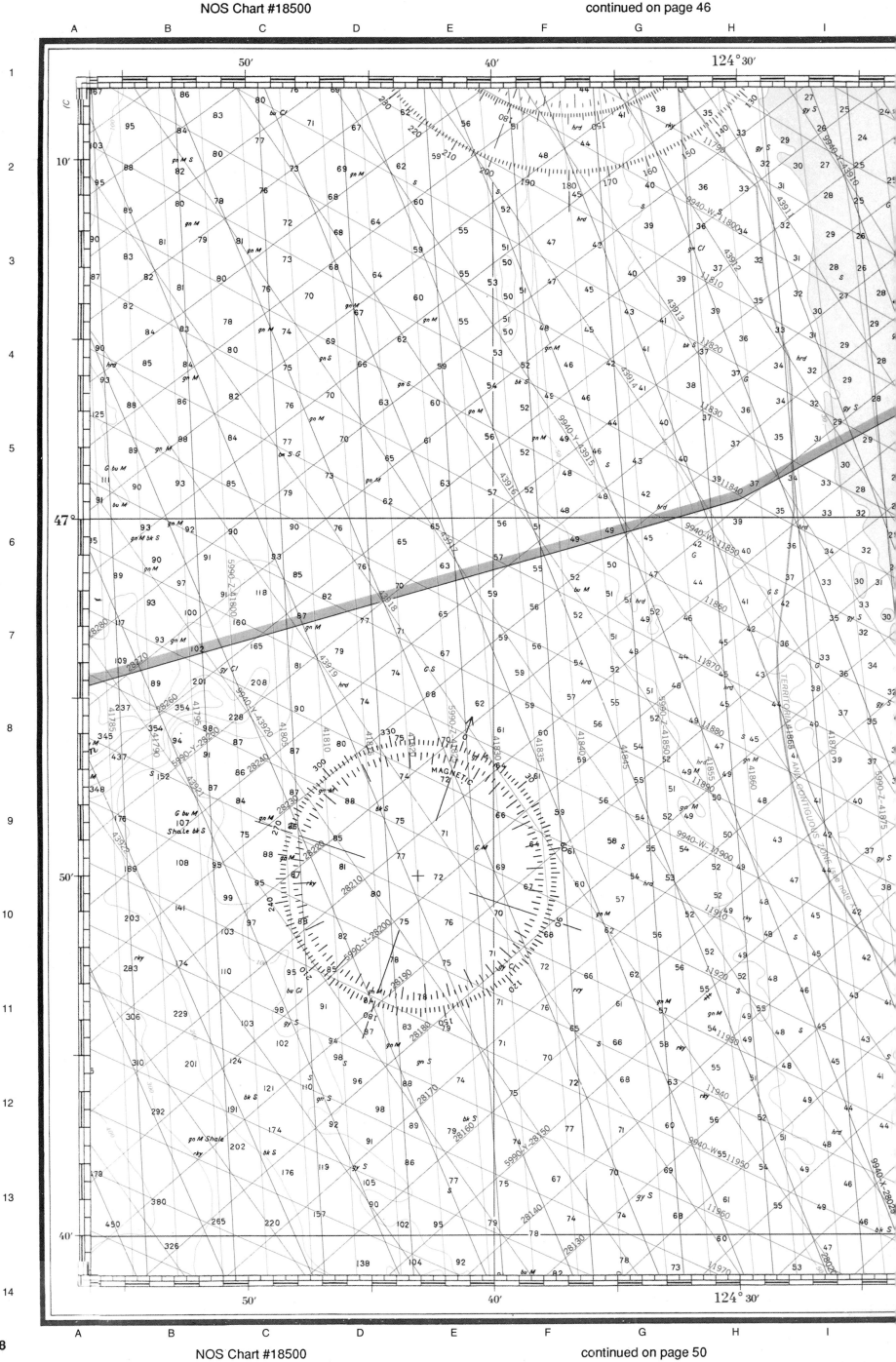

continued on page 50

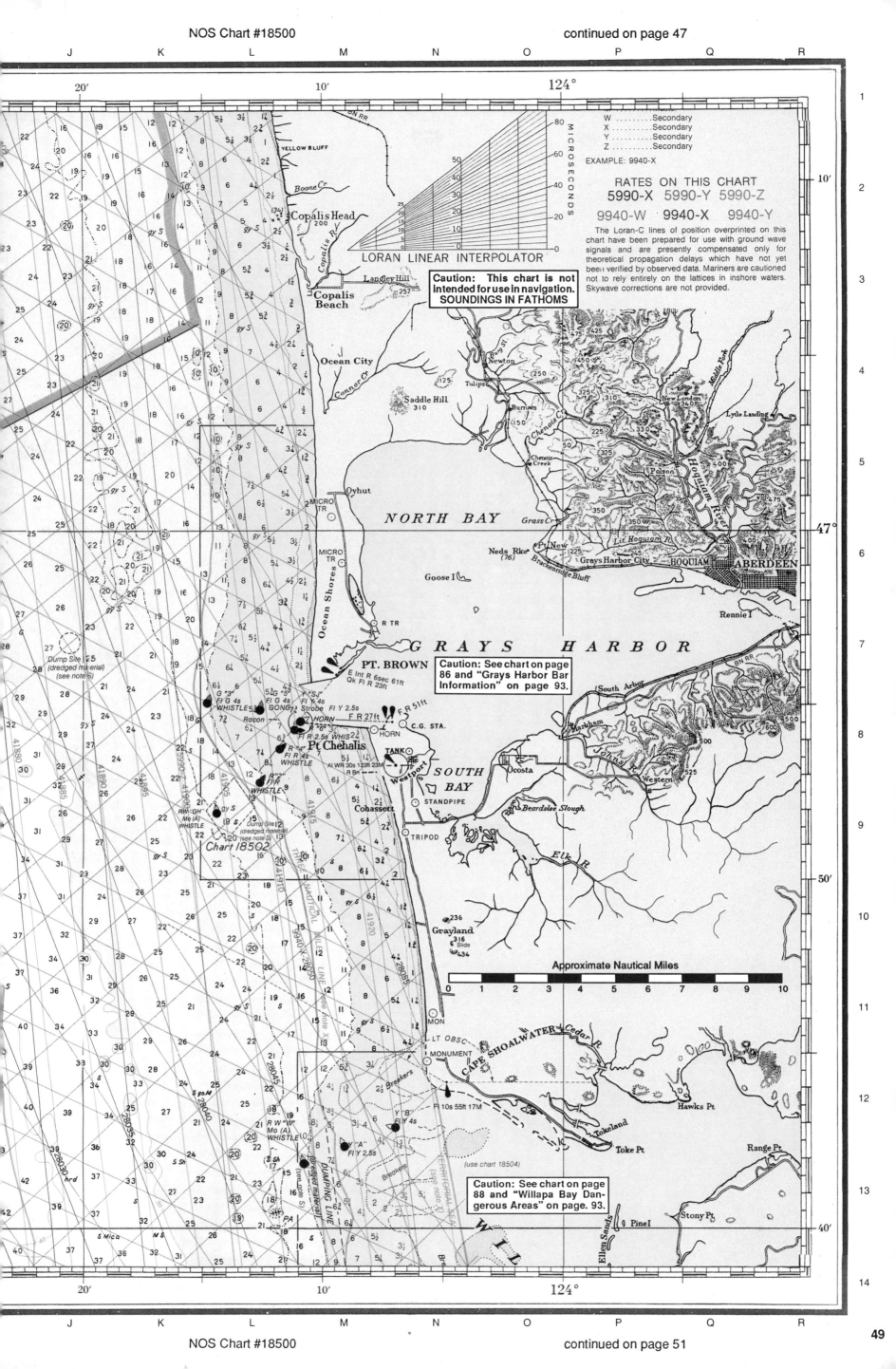

Caution: This chart is not intended for use in navigation. SOUNDINGS IN FATHOMS

RATES ON THIS CHART
5990-X 5990-Y 5990-Z
9940-W 9940-X 9940-Y

The Loran-C lines of position overprinted on this chart have been prepared for use with ground wave signals and are presently compensated only for theoretical propagation delays which have not yet been verified by observed data. Mariners are cautioned not to rely entirely on the lattices in inshore waters. Skywave corrections are not provided.

W .... Master
X .... Secondary
Y .... Secondary
Z .... Secondary
EXAMPLE: 9940-X

LORAN LINEAR INTERPOLATOR

Caution: See chart on page 86 and "Grays Harbor Bar Information" on page 93.

Caution: See chart on page 88 and "Willapa Bay Dangerous Areas" on page. 93.

Approximate Nautical Miles

NORTH BAY

GRAYS HARBOR

SOUTH BAY

Chart 18502

continued on page 48

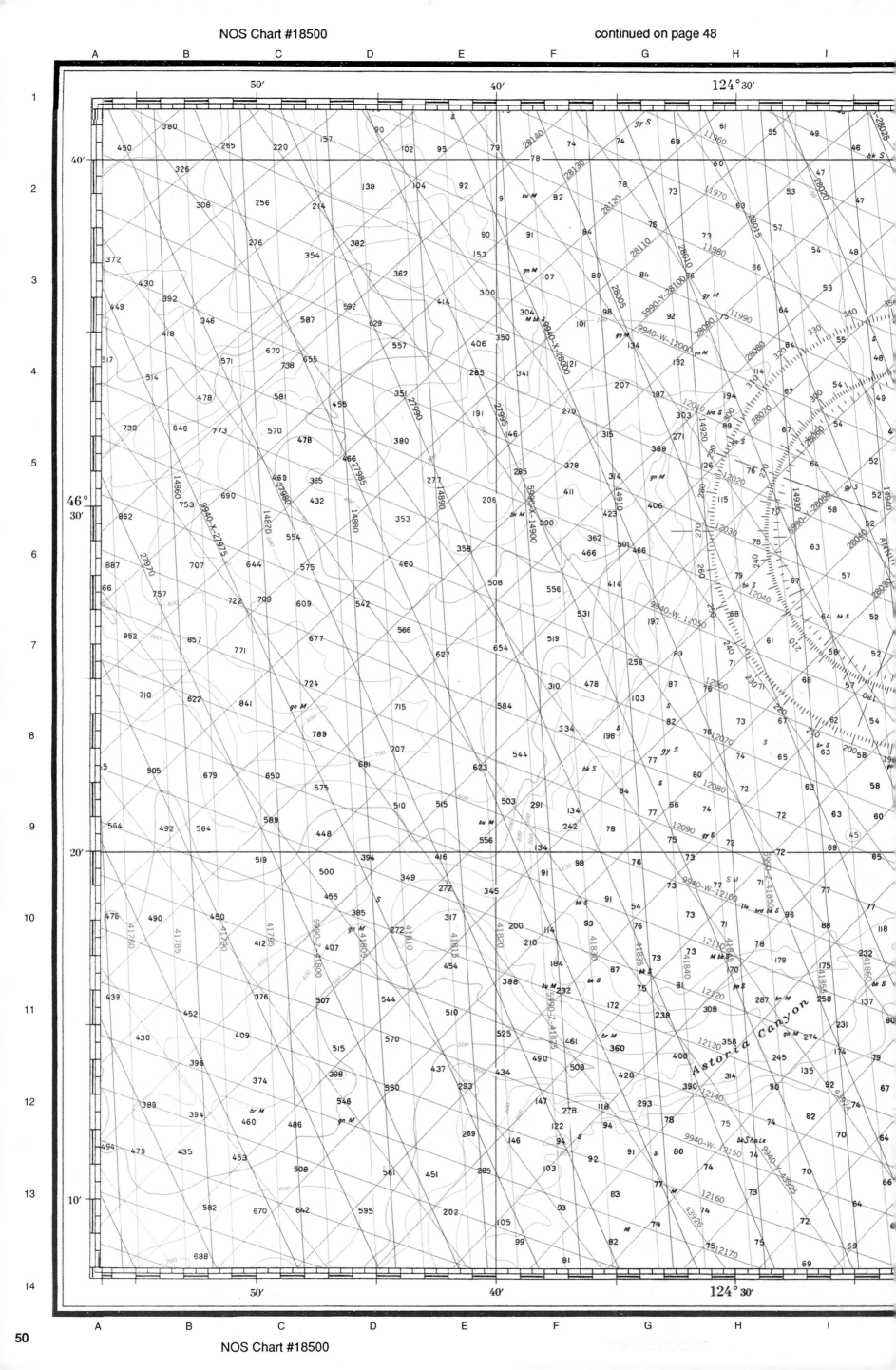

continued on page 49

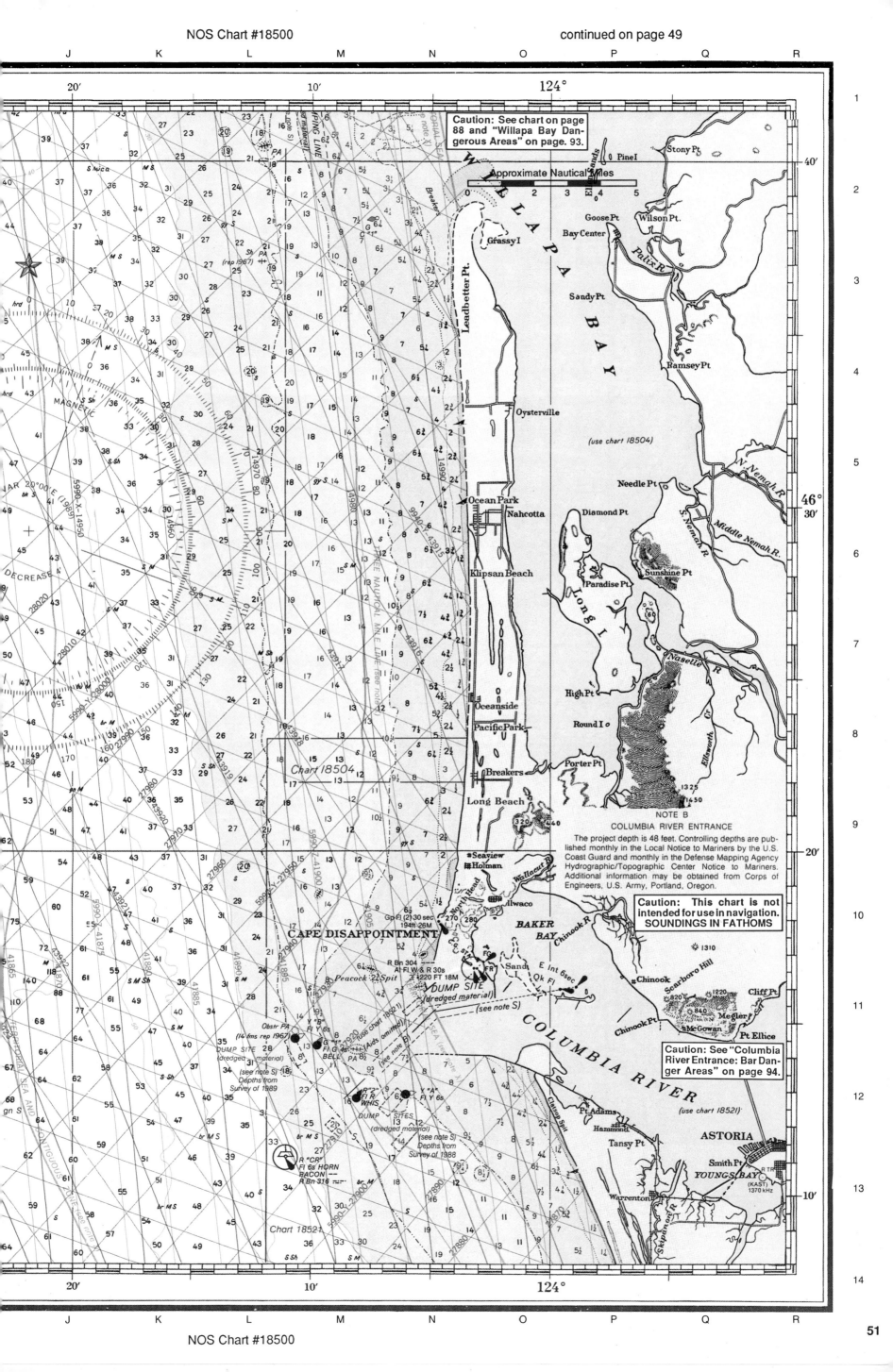

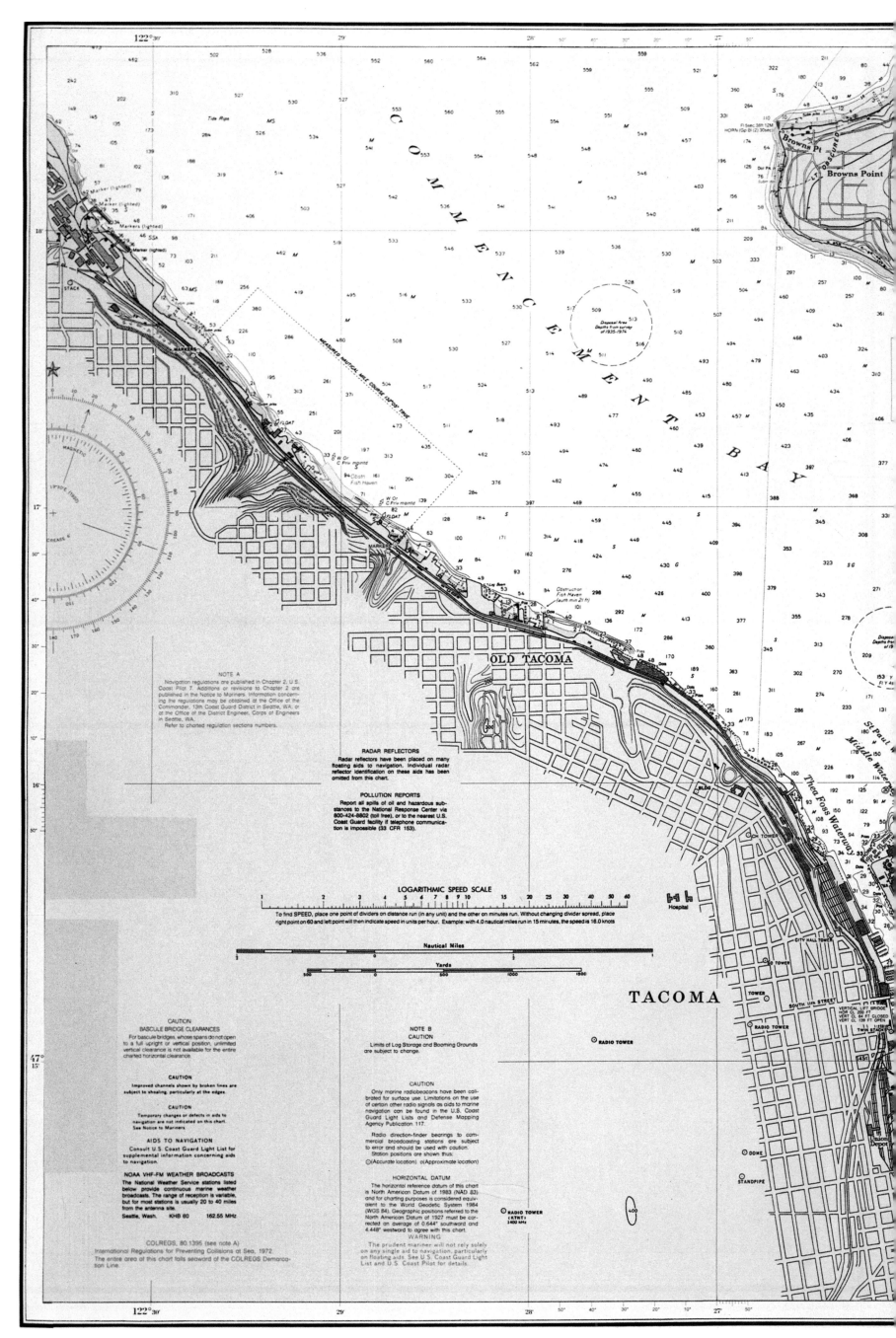

NOS Chart #18453

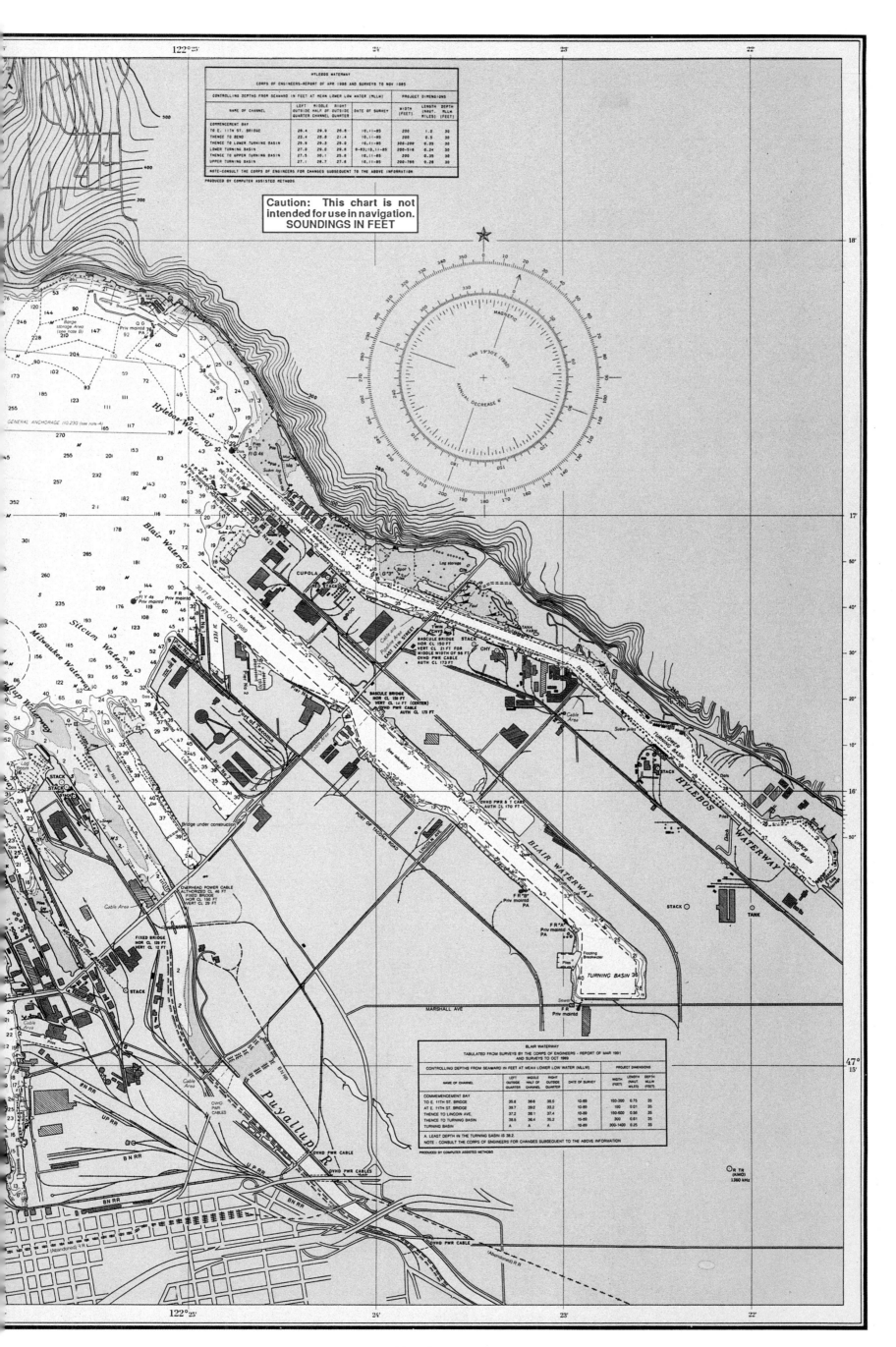

Caution: This chart is not
intended for use in navigation.
SOUNDINGS IN FEET

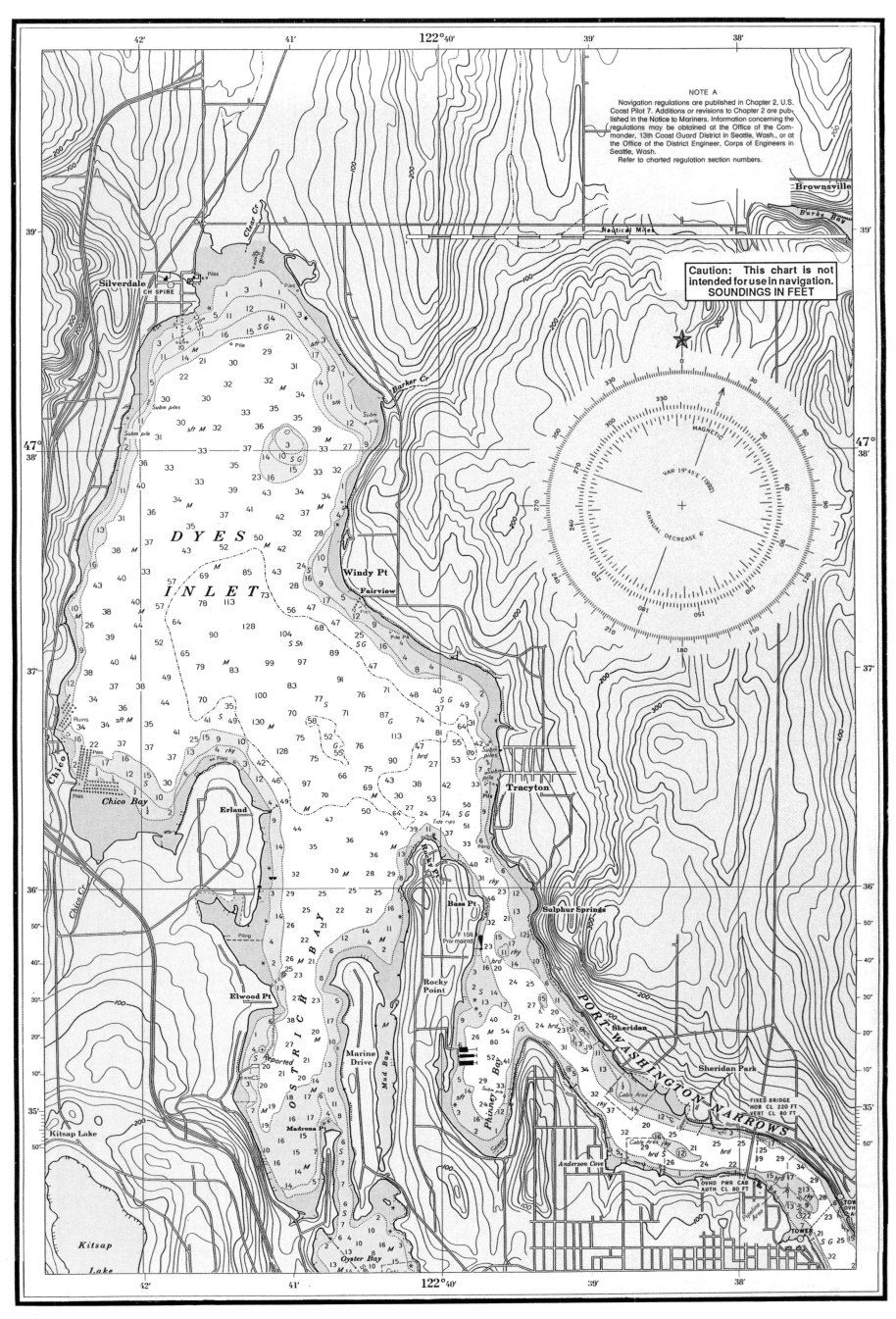

NOTE A
Navigation regulations are published in Chapter 2, U.S. Coast Pilot 7. Additions or revisions to Chapter 2 are published in the Notice to Mariners. Information concerning the regulations may be obtained at the Office of the Commander, 13th Coast Guard District in Seattle, Wash., or at the Office of the District Engineer, Corps of Engineers in Seattle, Wash.
Refer to charted regulation section numbers.

Caution: This chart is not intended for use in navigation. SOUNDINGS IN FEET

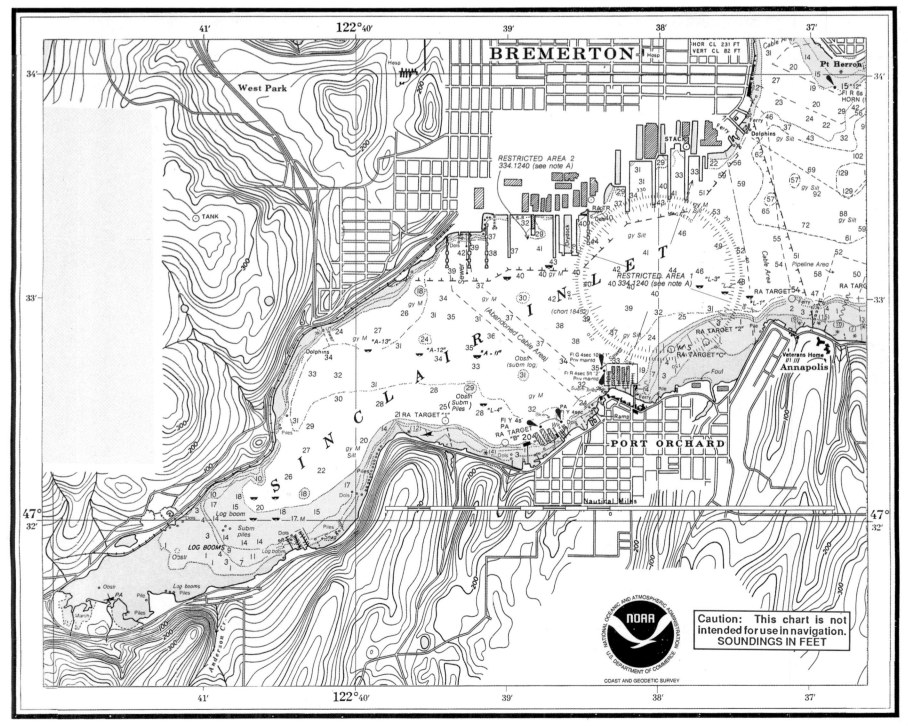

NOS Chart #18449

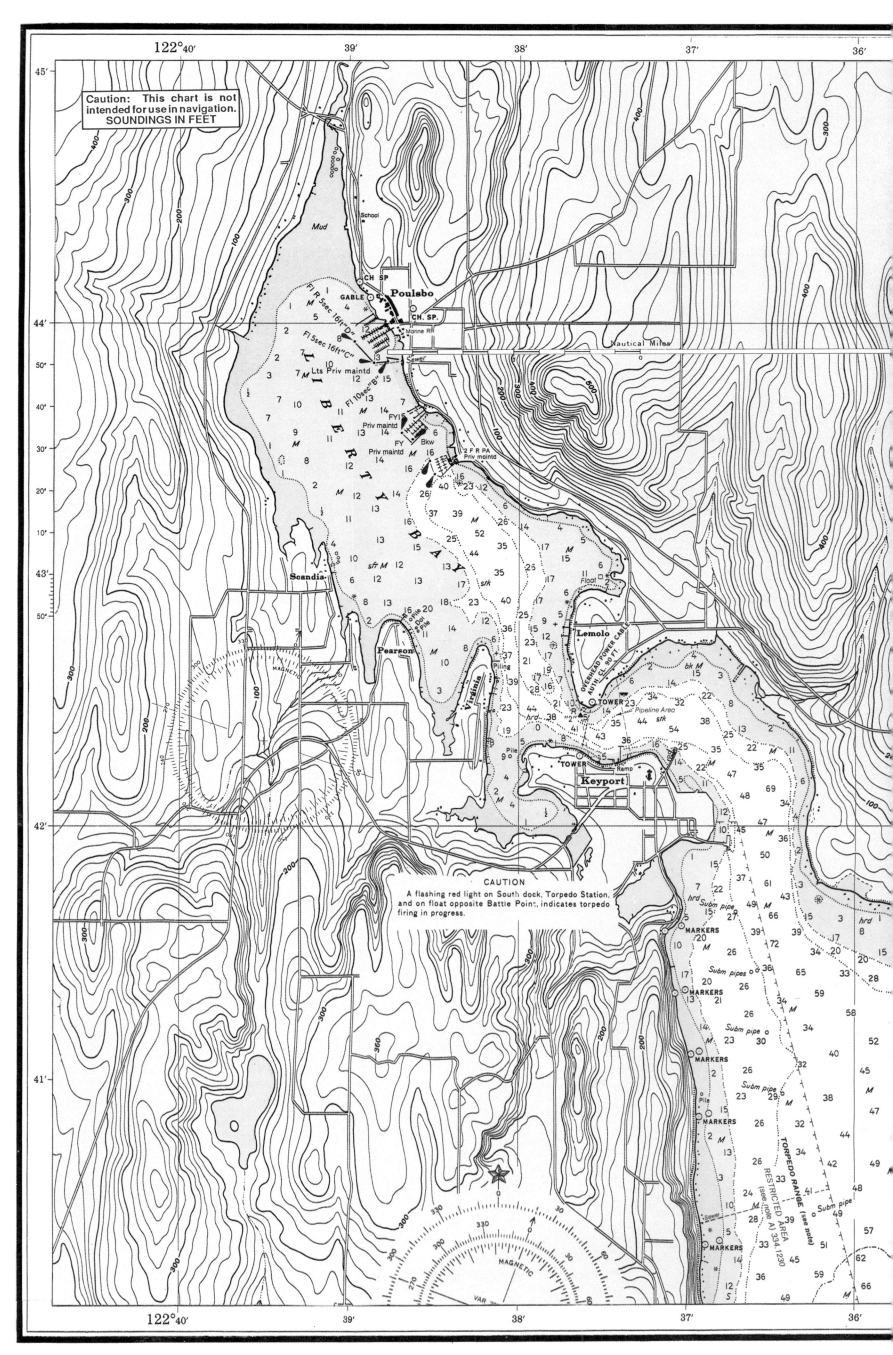

Caution: This chart is not intended for use in navigation. SOUNDINGS IN FEET

122°40'

45'

Mud

School

CH SP
GABLE
Poulsbo
CH. SP.

Fl R 5sec 16ft "D"

44'
Fl 5sec 16ft "C"
Marine RR

Lts Priv maintd
Sewer

L
I
B
E
R
T
Y

Fl 10sec "B"

FY
Priv maintd

FY Bkw
Priv maintd

2 F R PA
Priv maintd

B
A
Y

Nautical Miles

Scandia

Float

Lemolo

Overhead Power Cable
AUTH. CL 50 FT

Pearson

Virginia

TOWER
R
Pipeline Area

Pile

TOWER
Ramp
Keyport

CAUTION
A flashing red light on South dock, Torpedo Station,
and on float opposite Battle Point, indicates torpedo
firing in progress.

MARKERS

Subm pipe

MARKERS

Subm pipes

MARKERS

Subm pipe

MARKERS

Subm pipe

MAGNETIC

MARKERS

TORPEDO RANGE
RESTRICTED AREA (see note)
(see note A) 334, 1230

Subm pipe

MAGNETIC

VAR

122°40'   39'   38'   37'   36'

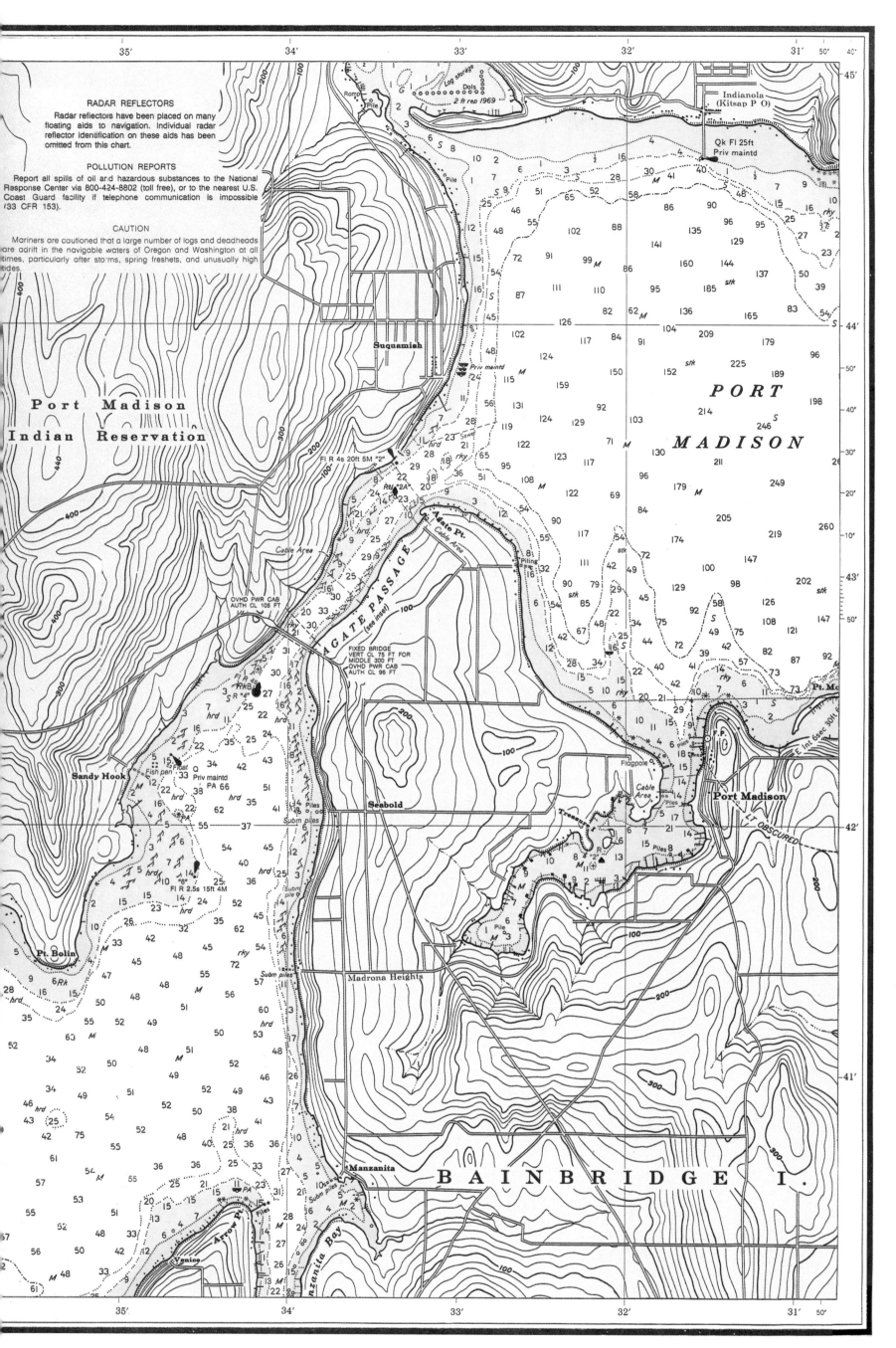

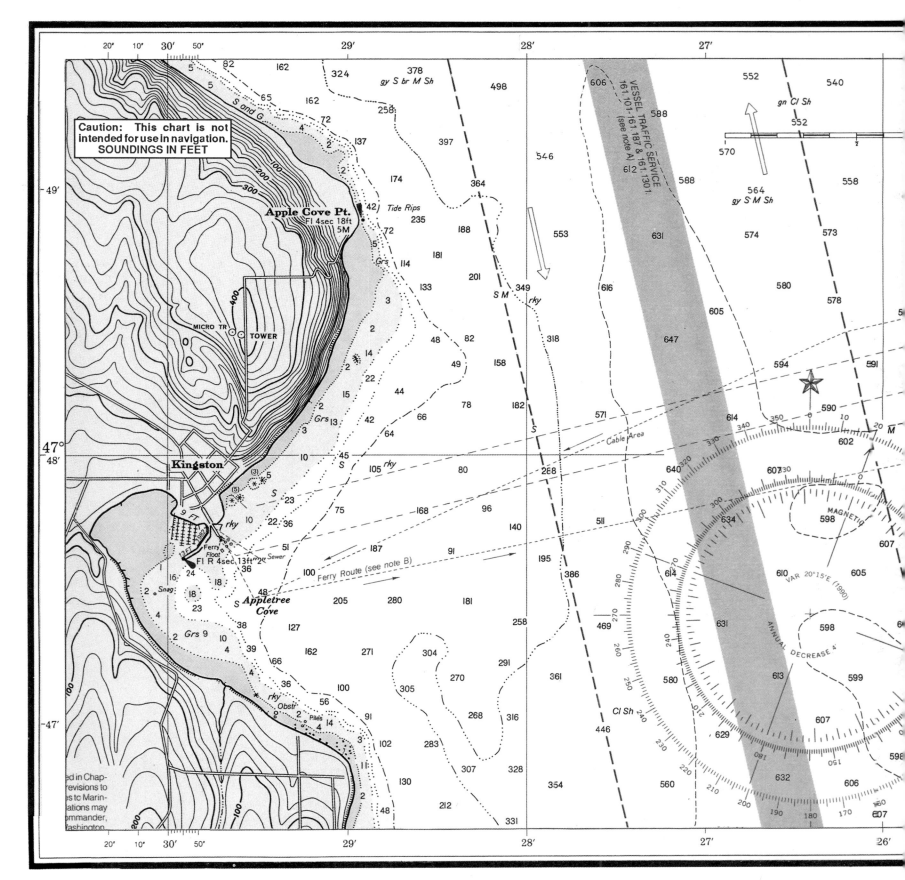

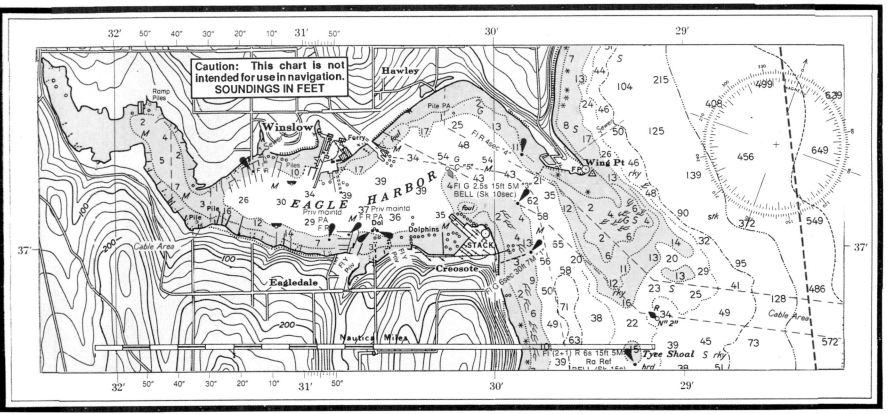

NOS Chart #18449

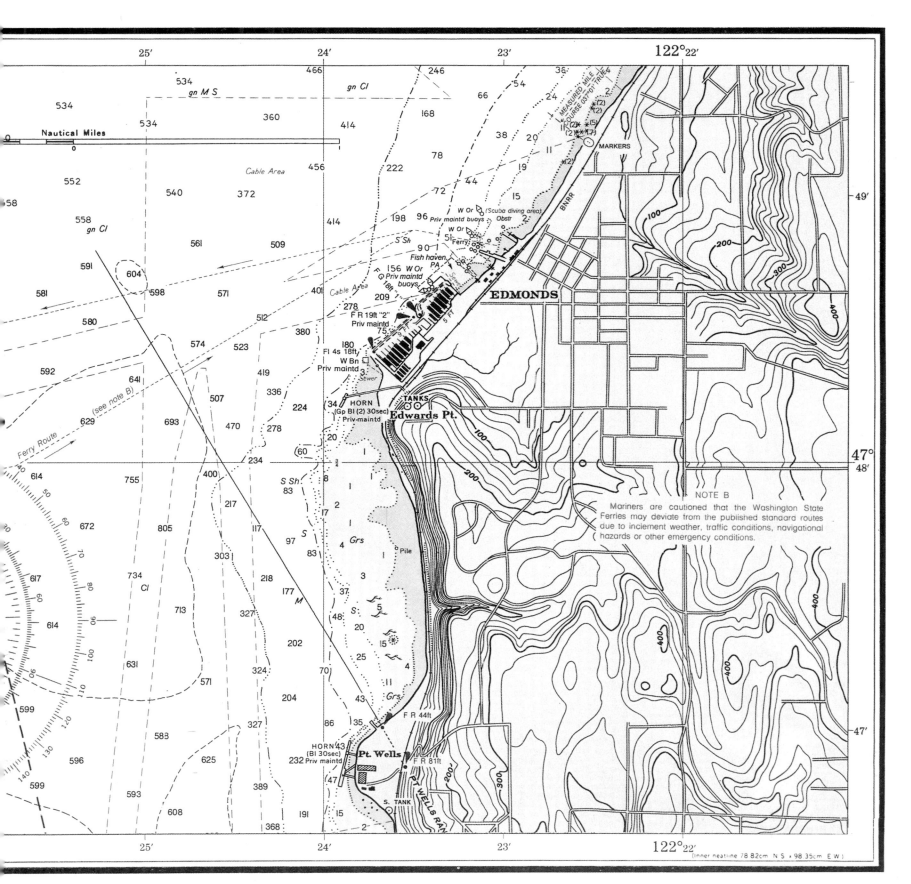

NOS Chart #18446

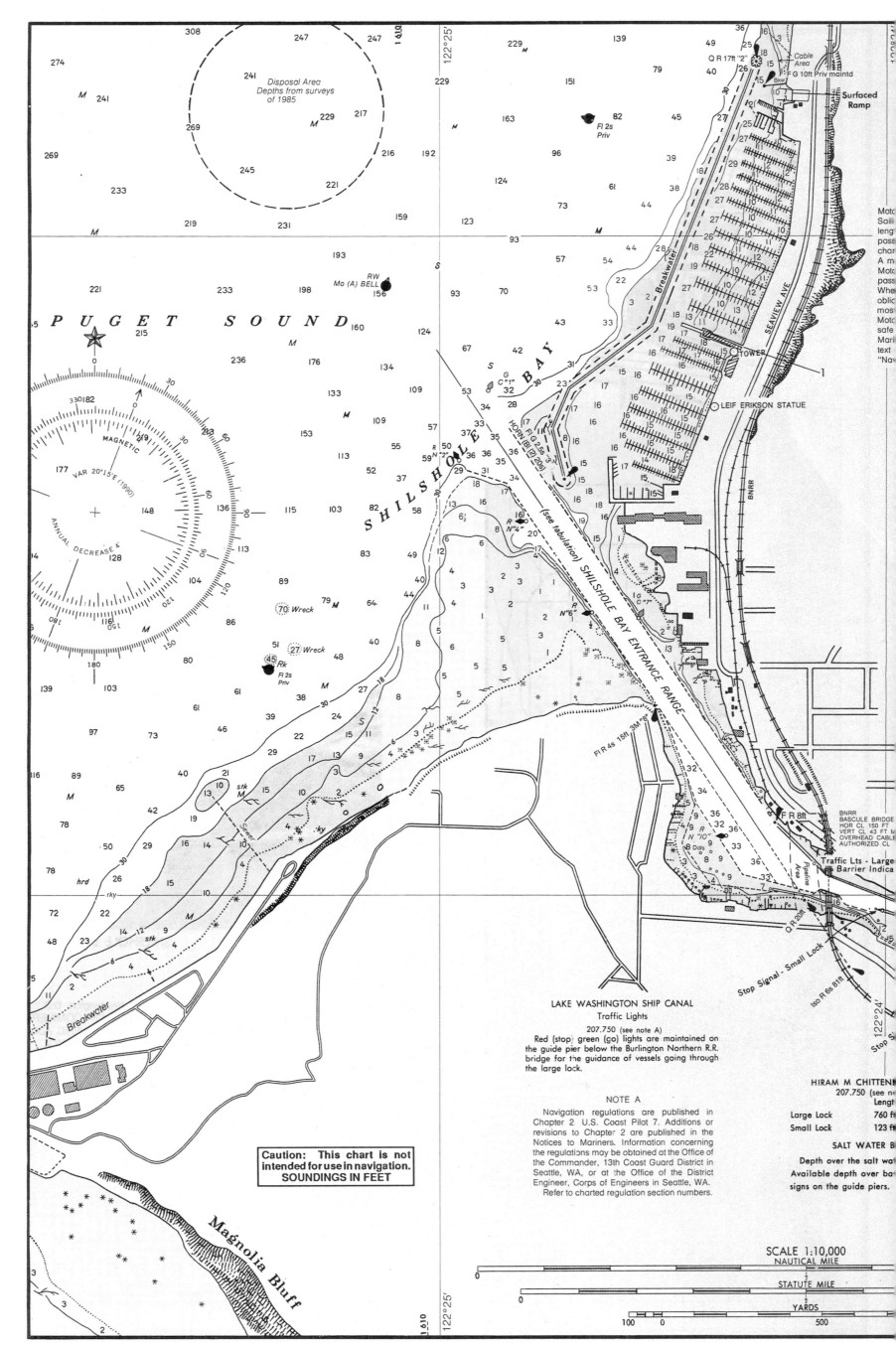

NOS Chart #18447

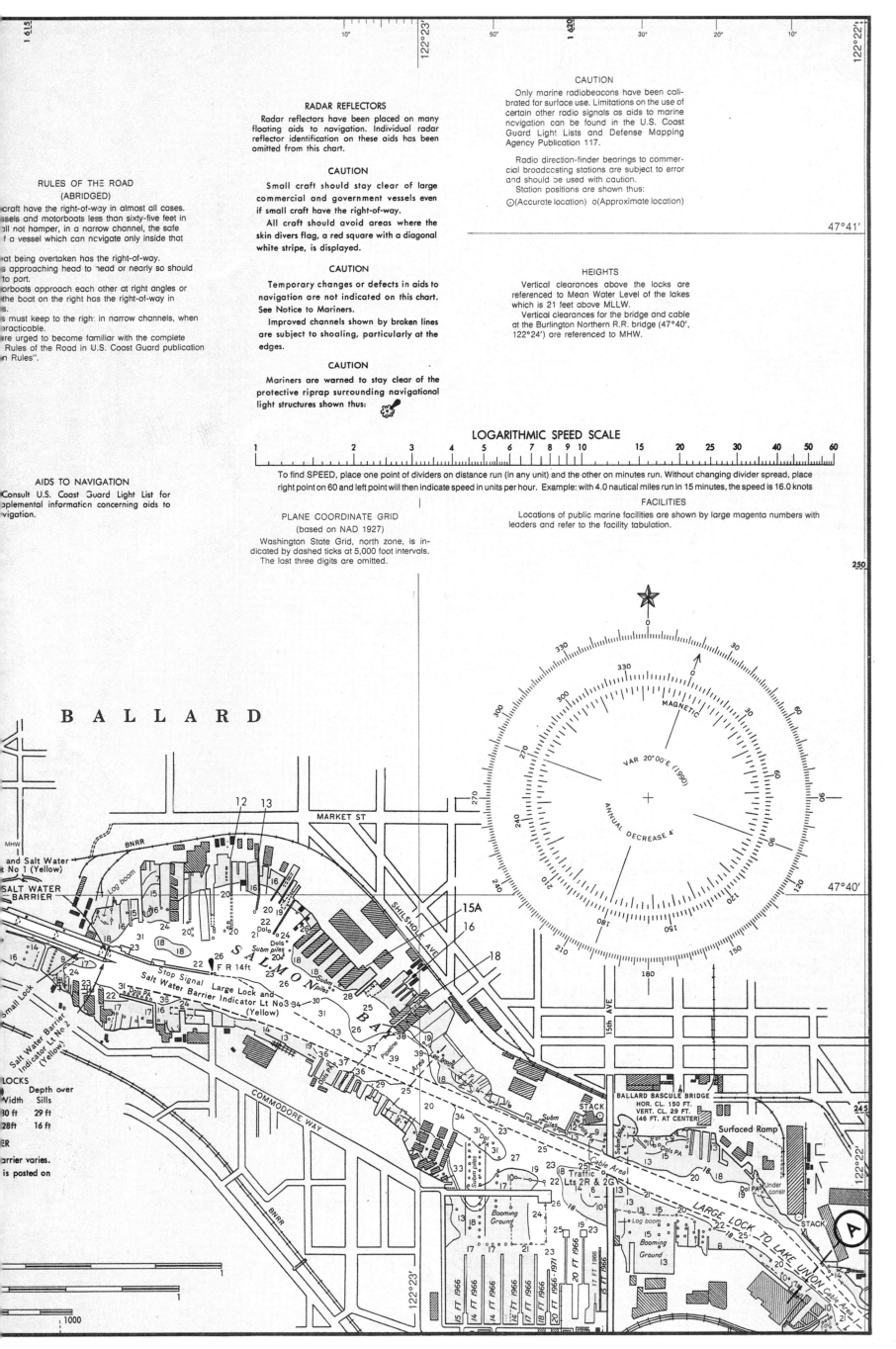

RULES OF THE ROAD
(ABRIDGED)

craft have the right-of-way in almost all cases.
ssels and motorboats less than sixty-five feet in
ill not hamper, in a narrow channel, the safe
f a vessel which can navigate only inside that

at being overtaken has the right-of-way.
s approaching head to head or nearly so should
to port.
orboats approach each other at right angles or
the boat on the right has the right-of-way in
s.
s must keep to the right in narrow channels, when
racticable.
re urged to become familiar with the complete
Rules of the Road in U.S. Coast Guard publication
n Rules".

AIDS TO NAVIGATION

Consult U.S. Coast Guard Light List for
pplemental information concerning aids to
vigation.

RADAR REFLECTORS

Radar reflectors have been placed on many
floating aids to navigation. Individual radar
reflector identification on these aids has been
omitted from this chart.

CAUTION

Small craft should stay clear of large
commercial and government vessels even
if small craft have the right-of-way.

All craft should avoid areas where the
skin divers flag, a red square with a diagonal
white stripe, is displayed.

CAUTION

Temporary changes or defects in aids to
navigation are not indicated on this chart.
See Notice to Mariners.

Improved channels shown by broken lines
are subject to shoaling, particularly at the
edges.

CAUTION

Mariners are warned to stay clear of the
protective riprap surrounding navigational
light structures shown thus:

CAUTION

Only marine radiobeacons have been calibrated for surface use. Limitations on the use of
certain other radio signals as aids to marine
navigation can be found in the U.S. Coast
Guard Light Lists and Defense Mapping
Agency Publication 117.

Radio direction-finder bearings to commercial broadcasting stations are subject to error
and should be used with caution.
Station positions are shown thus:
⊙(Accurate location) o(Approximate location)

HEIGHTS

Vertical clearances above the locks are
referenced to Mean Water Level of the lakes
which is 21 feet above MLLW.

Vertical clearances for the bridge and cable
at the Burlington Northern R.R. bridge (47°40',
122°24') are referenced to MHW.

LOGARITHMIC SPEED SCALE

To find SPEED, place one point of dividers on distance run (in any unit) and the other on minutes run. Without changing divider spread, place
right point on 60 and left point will then indicate speed in units per hour. Example: with 4.0 nautical miles run in 15 minutes, the speed is 16.0 knots

PLANE COORDINATE GRID
(based on NAD 1927)

Washington State Grid, north zone, is indicated by dashed ticks at 5,000 foot intervals.
The last three digits are omitted.

FACILITIES

Locations of public marine facilities are shown by large magenta numbers with
leaders and refer to the facility tabulation.

B A L L A R D

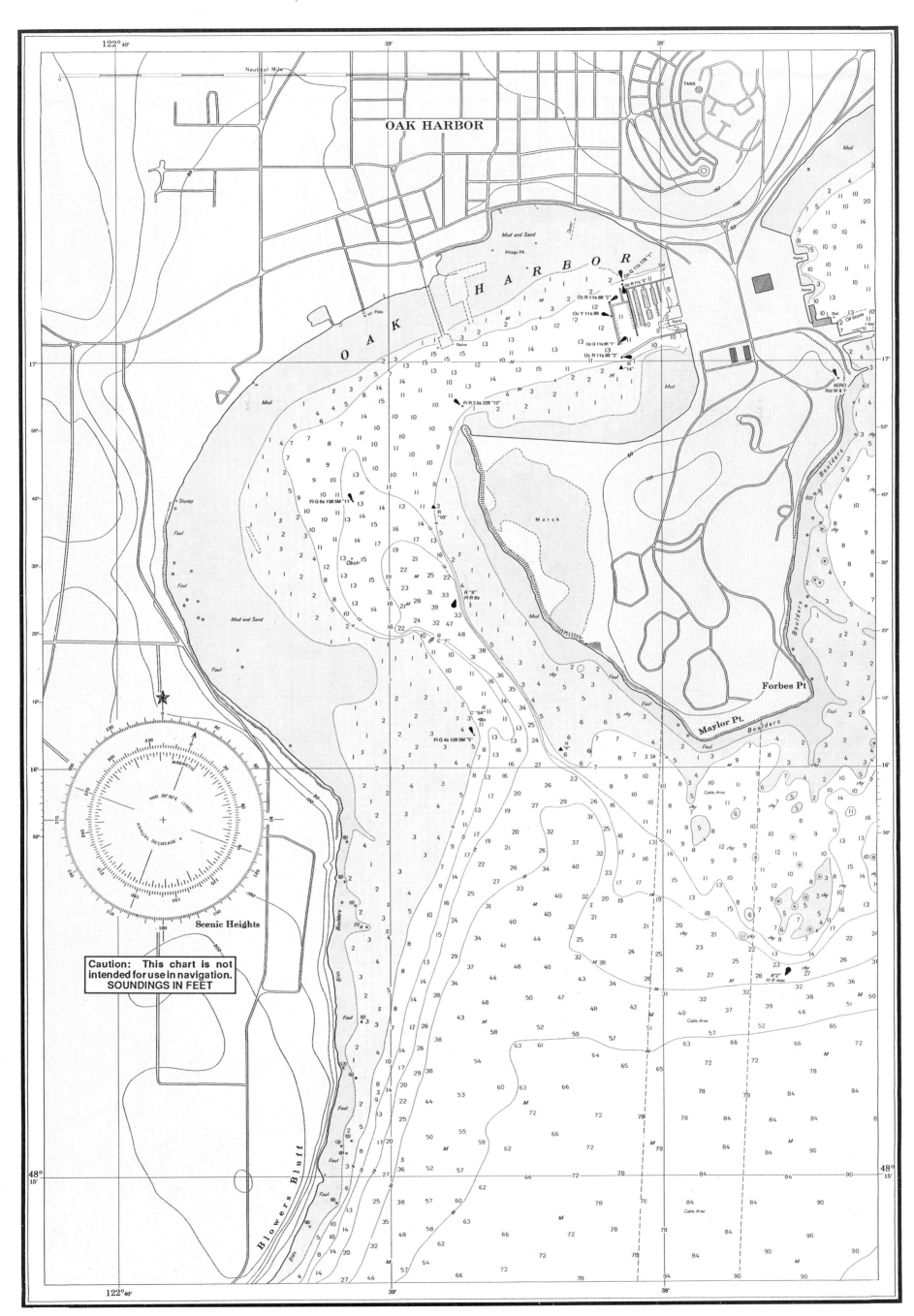

OAK HARBOR

Caution: This chart is not intended for use in navigation. SOUNDINGS IN FEET

Scenic Heights

Blowers Bluff

Forbes Pt.

Maylor Pt.

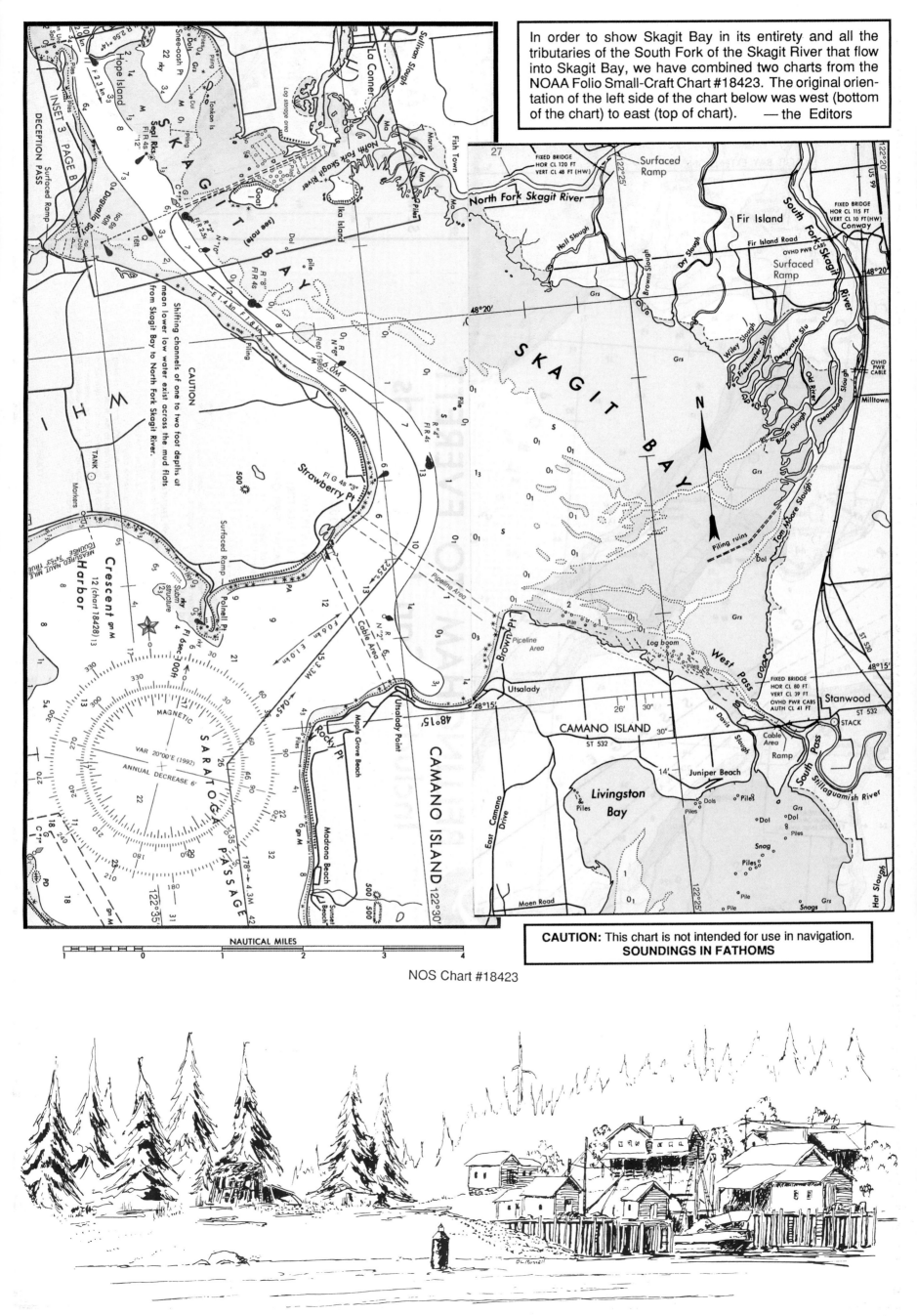

In order to show Skagit Bay in its entirety and all the tributaries of the South Fork of the Skagit River that flow into Skagit Bay, we have combined two charts from the NOAA Folio Small-Craft Chart #18423. The original orientation of the left side of the chart below was west (bottom of the chart) to east (top of chart).   — the Editors

CAUTION: This chart is not intended for use in navigation.
SOUNDINGS IN FATHOMS

NOS Chart #18423

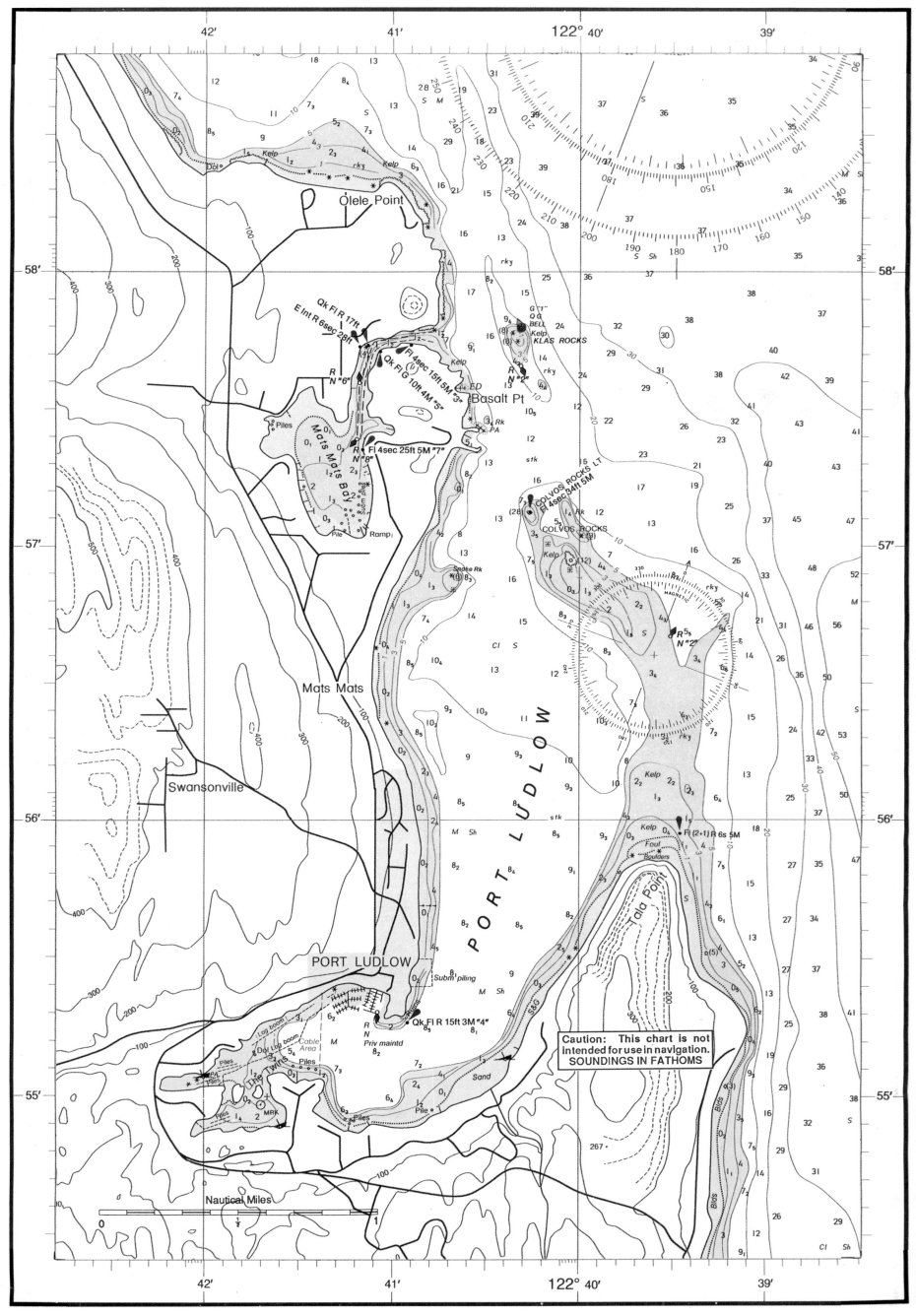

Caution: This chart is not
intended for use in navigation.
SOUNDINGS IN FATHOMS

PORT LUDLOW

Olele Point

Basalt Pt

KLAS ROCKS

COLVOS ROCKS LT
Fl 4sec 34ft 5M
COLVOS ROCKS

Mats Mats Bay

Mats Mats

Swansonville

Tala Point

PORT LUDLOW

The Twins

Nautical Miles

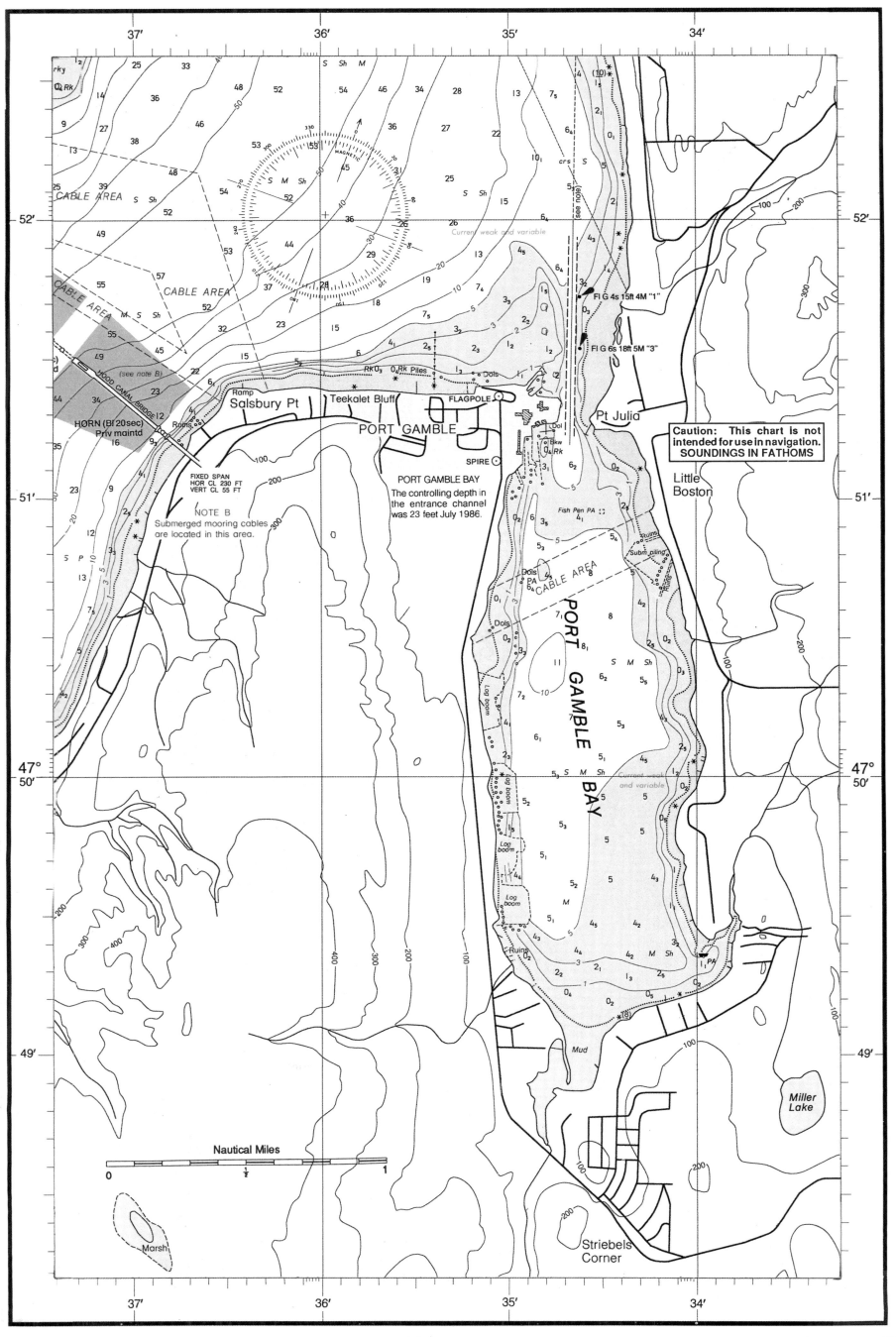

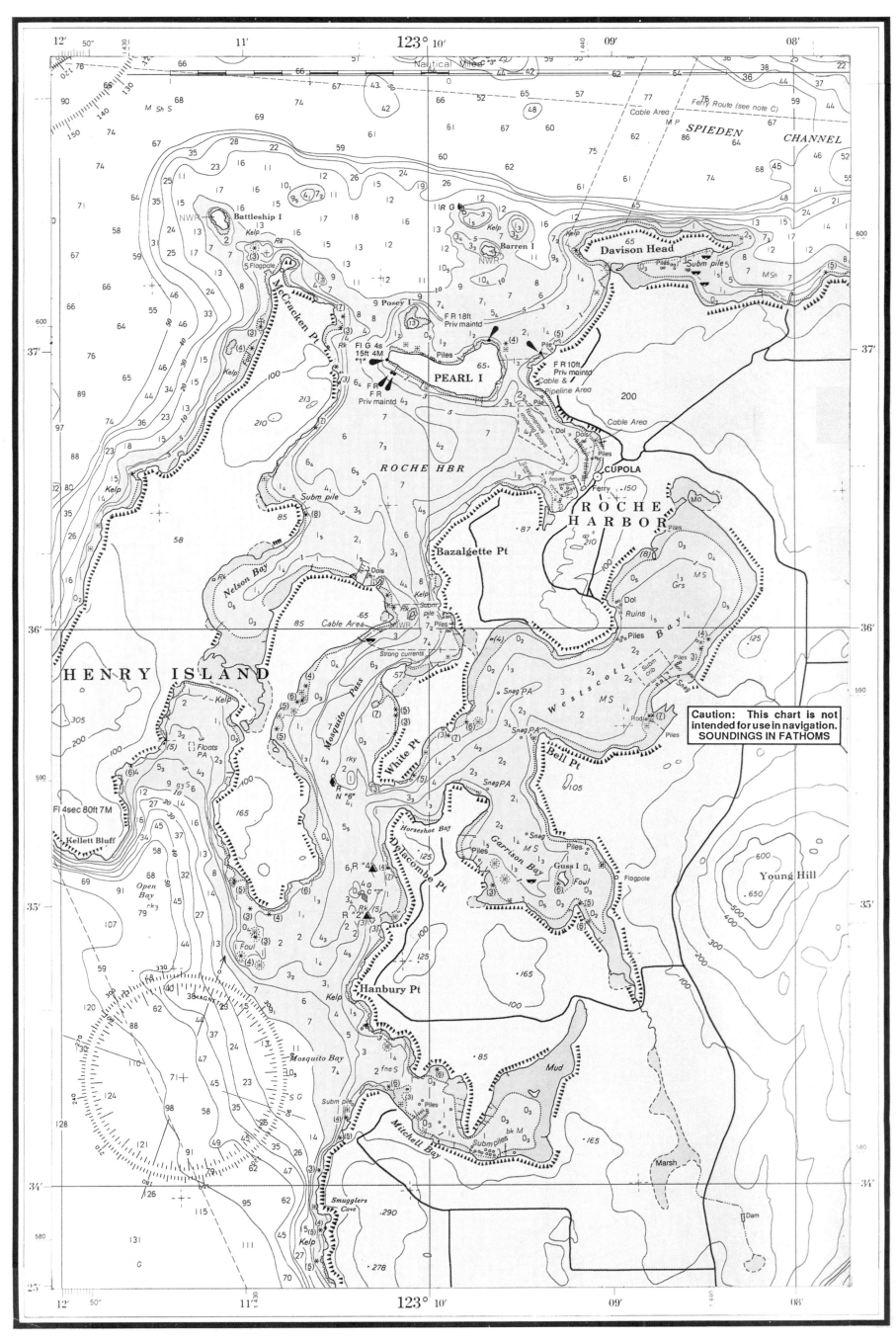

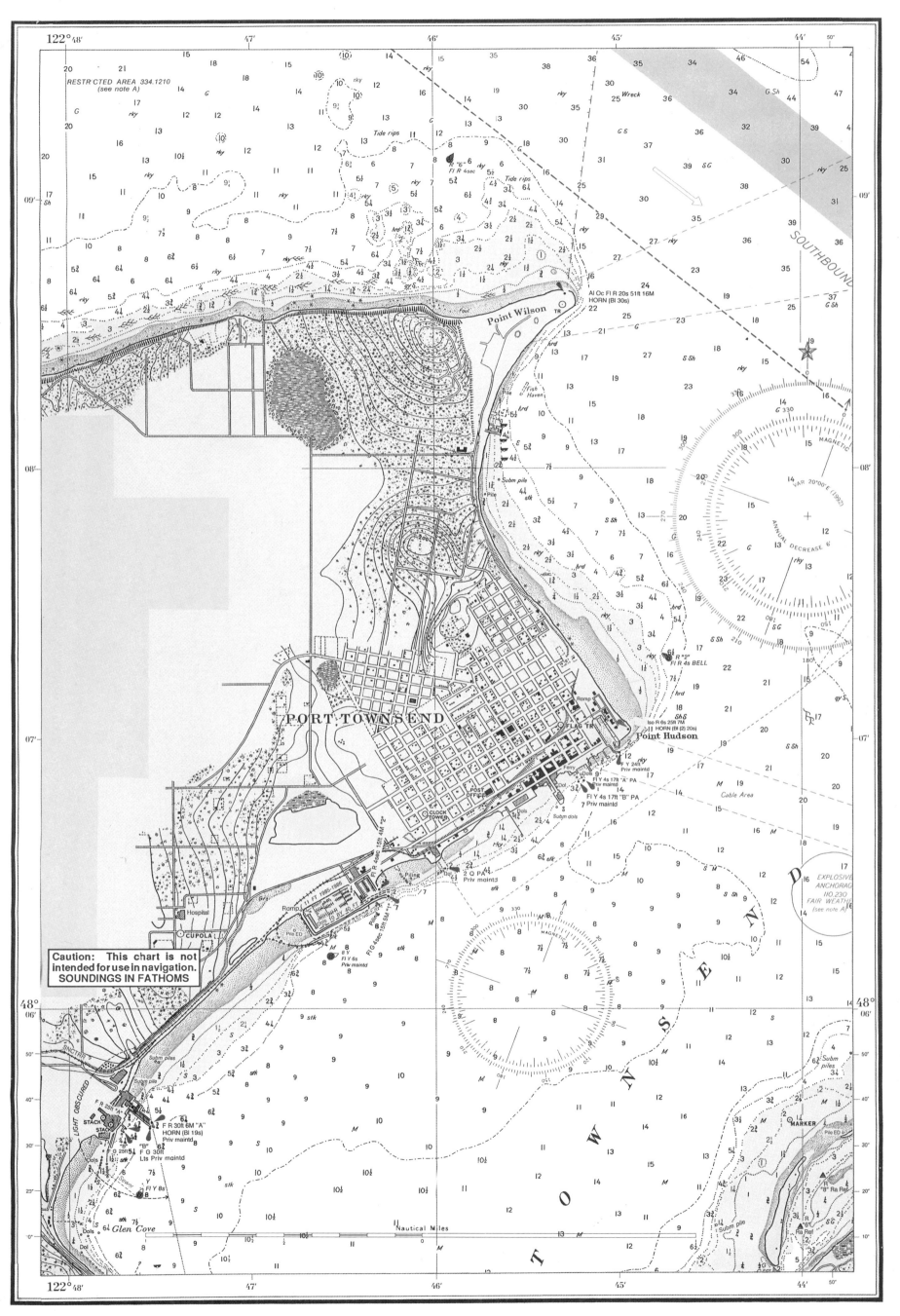

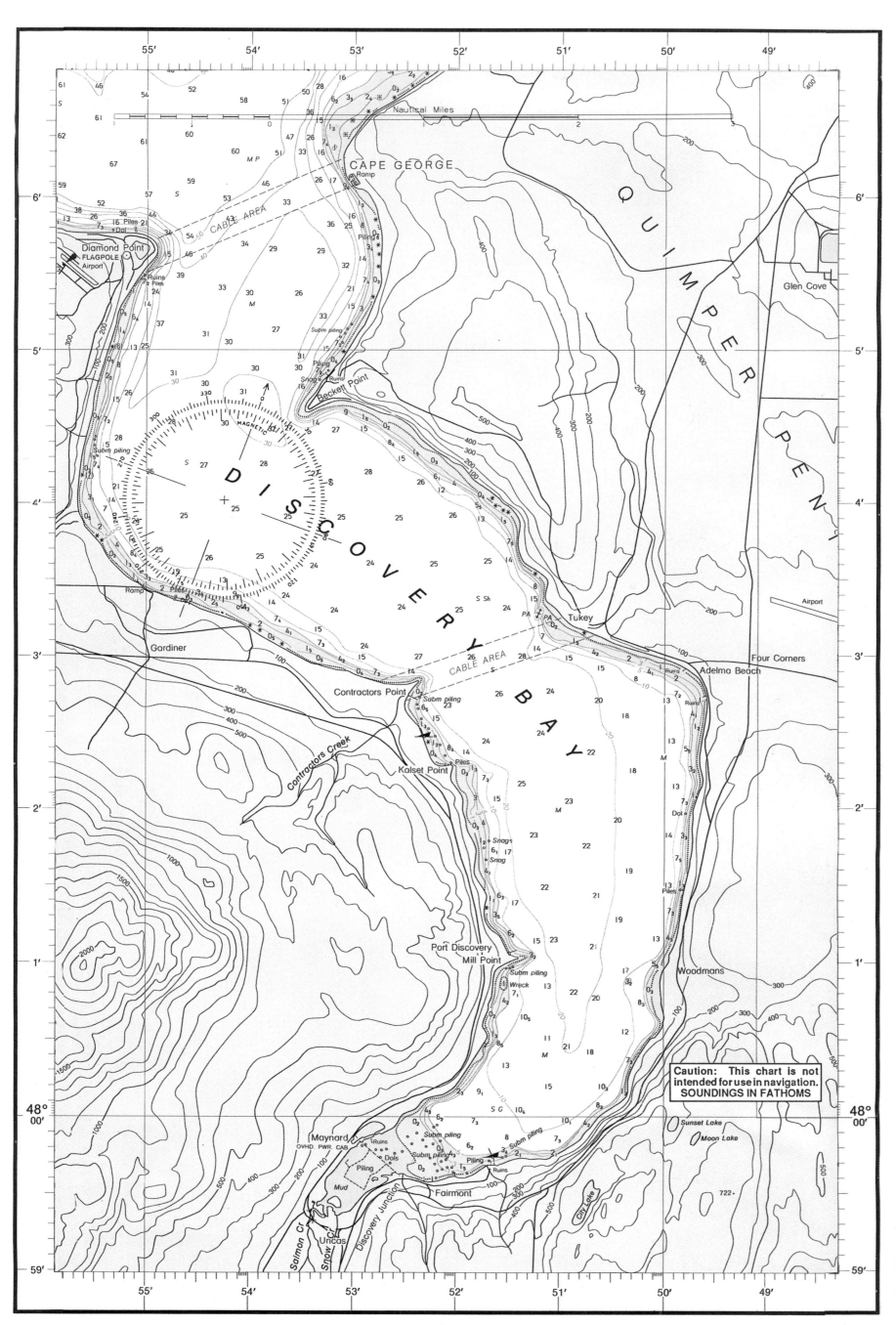

NOS Chart #18471

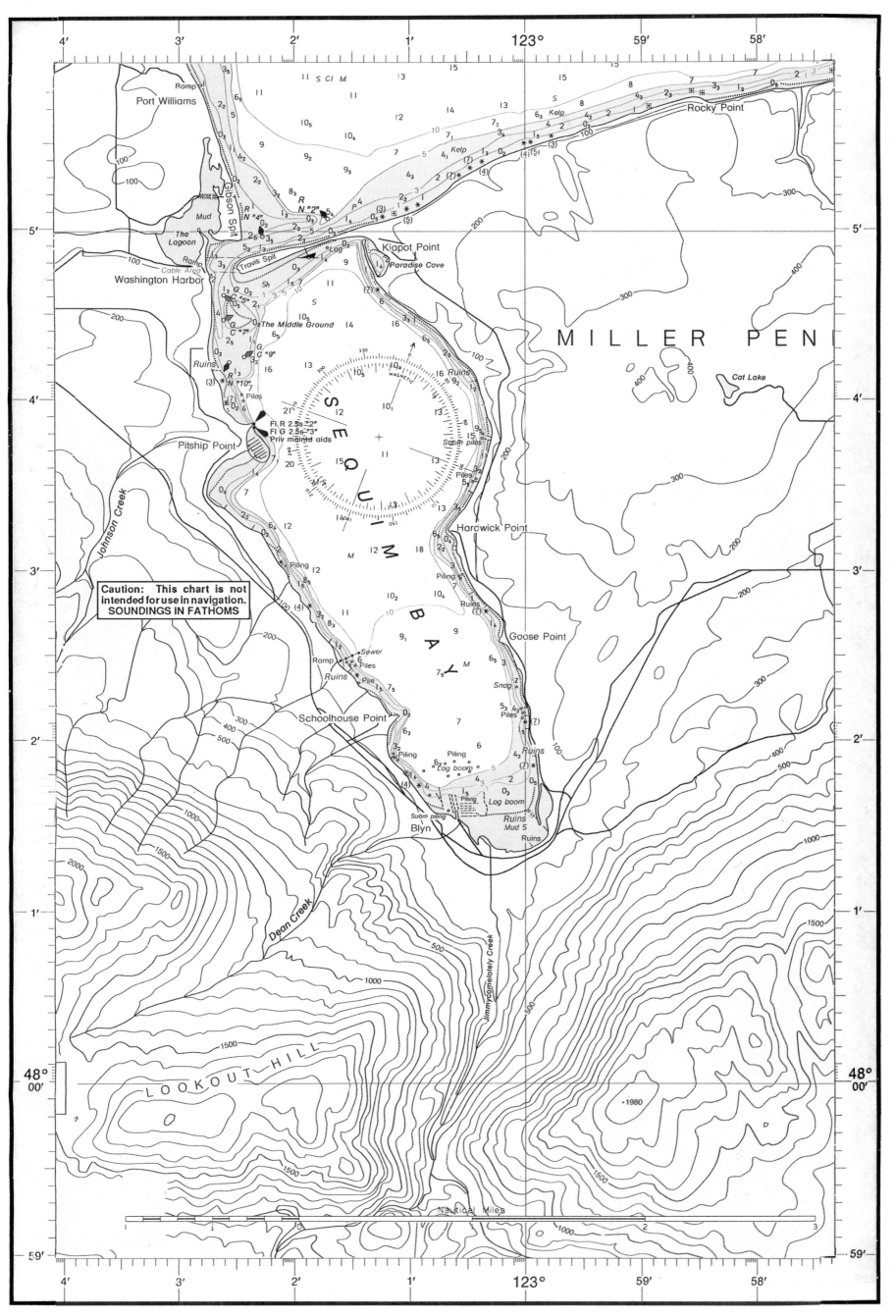

Caution: This chart is not
intended for use in navigation.
SOUNDINGS IN FATHOMS

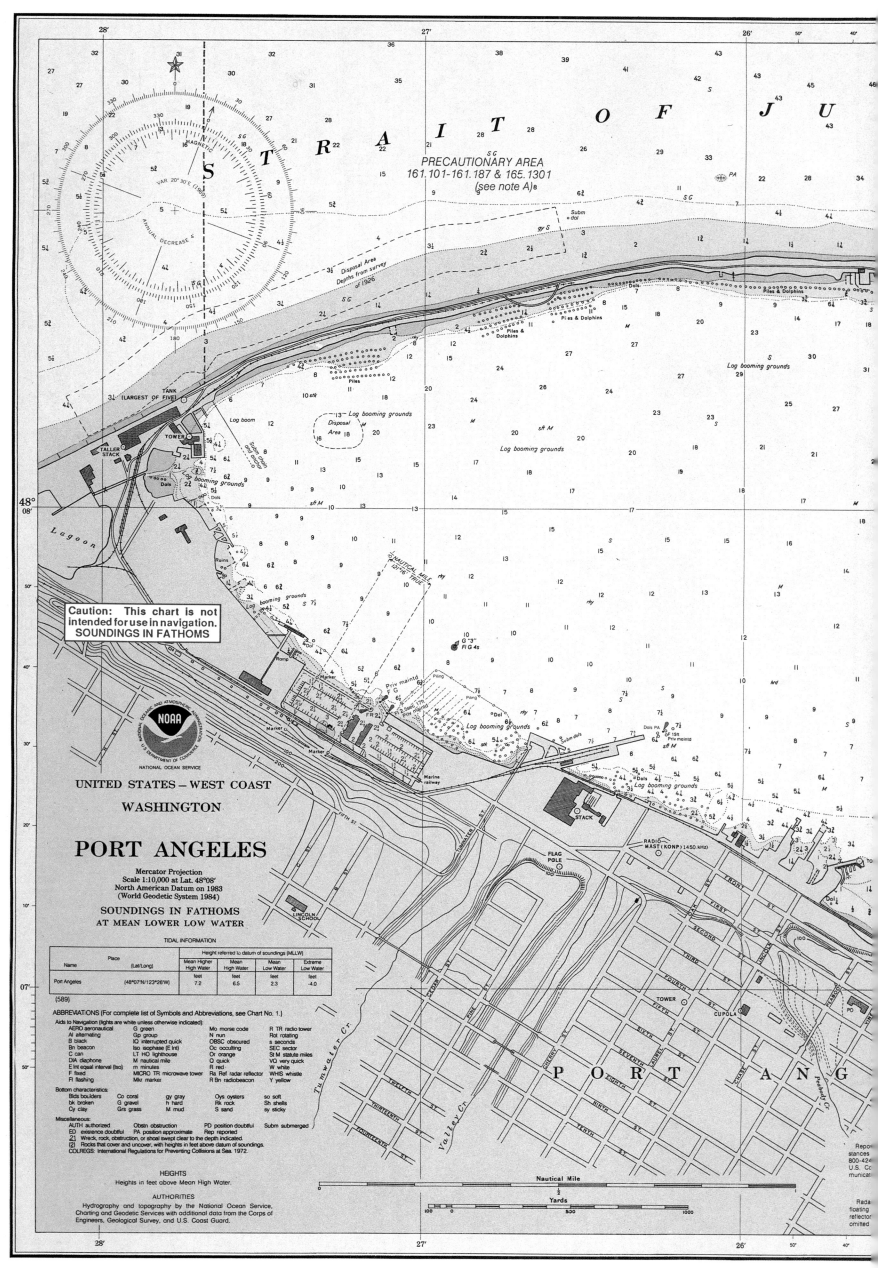

**Caution: This chart is not intended for use in navigation.
SOUNDINGS IN FATHOMS**

UNITED STATES — WEST COAST

WASHINGTON

PORT ANGELES

Mercator Projection
Scale 1:10,000 at Lat. 48°08'
North American Datum on 1983
(World Geodetic System 1984)

SOUNDINGS IN FATHOMS
AT MEAN LOWER LOW WATER

TIDAL INFORMATION

Name	Place (Lat/Long)	Height referred to datum of soundings (MLLW)			
		Mean Higher High Water feet	Mean High Water feet	Mean Low Water feet	Extreme Low Water feet
Port Angeles	(48°07'N/123°26'W)	7.2	6.5	2.3	-4.0

(589)

ABBREVIATIONS (For complete list of Symbols and Abbreviations, see Chart No. 1.)

Aids to Navigation (lights are white unless otherwise indicated):

AERO aeronautical	G green	Mo morse code	R TR radio tower
Al alternating	Gp group	N nun	Rot rotating
B black	IQ interrupted quick	OBSC obscured	s seconds
Bn beacon	Iso isophase (E Int)	Oc occulting	SEC sector
C can	LT HO lighthouse	Or orange	St M statute miles
DIA diaphone	M nautical mile	Q quick	VQ very quick
E Int equal interval (Iso)	m minutes	R red	W white
F fixed	MICRO TR microwave tower	Ra Ref radar reflector	WHIS whistle
Fl flashing	Mkr marker	R Bn radiobeacon	Y yellow

Bottom characteristics:

Blds boulders	Co coral	gy gray	Oys oysters	so soft
bk broken	G gravel	h hard	Rk rock	Sh shells
Cy clay	Grs grass	M mud	S sand	sy sticky

Miscellaneous:
AUTH authorized Obstn obstruction PD position doubtful Subm submerged
ED existence doubtful PA position approximate Rep reported
21 Wreck, rock, obstruction, or shoal swept clear to the depth indicated.
(2) Rocks that cover and uncover, with heights in feet above datum of soundings.
COLREGS: International Regulations for Preventing Collisions at Sea, 1972.

HEIGHTS
Heights in feet above Mean High Water.

AUTHORITIES
Hydrography and topography by the National Ocean Service,
Charting and Geodetic Services with additional data from the Corps of
Engineers, Geological Survey, and U.S. Coast Guard.

NOS Chart #18468

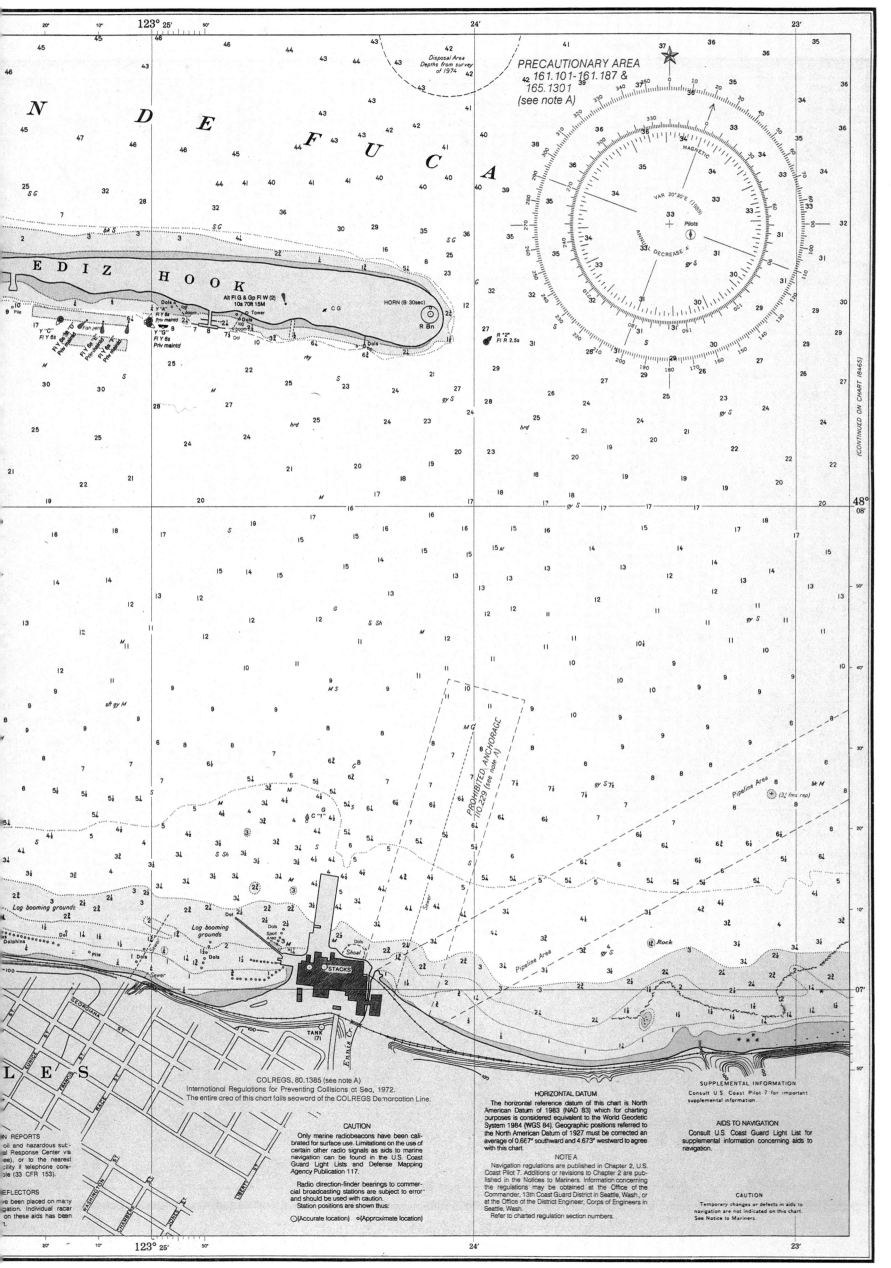

NOS Chart #18468

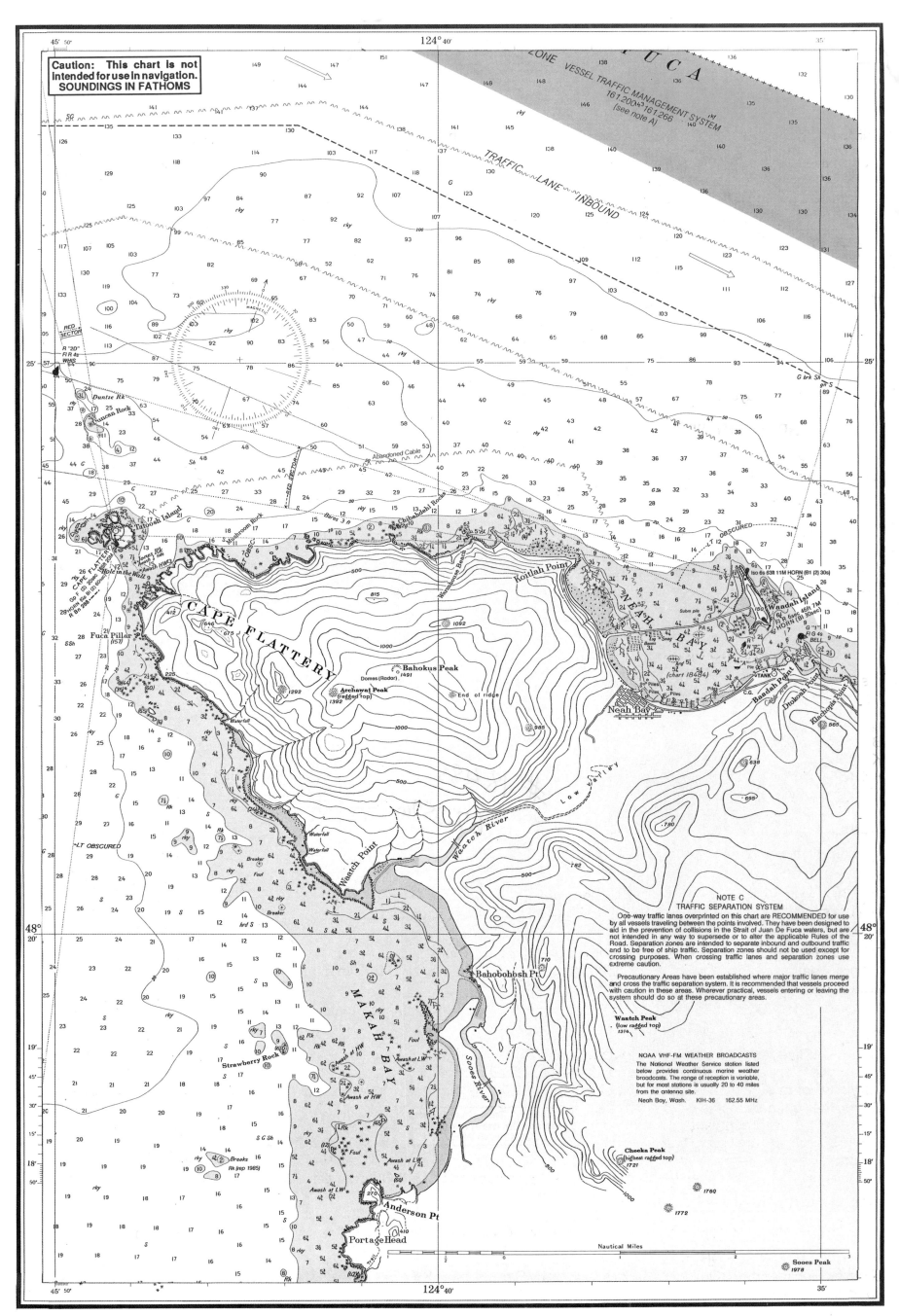

WILLAPA BAY DANGEROUS AREAS (See shaded areas on page 88.)

Most of the waters in the Willapa Bay entrance are "DANGEROUS AREAS". This is due to extensive shoal water, effects of ocean wind and swells, and the fact that bars and shoals are constantly changing. The sea can break into a dangerous surf at any time in this area. If your boat should swamp, help may not be able to reach you because the sea breaks into shoal water. The channel into Willapa Bay is subject to frequent changes.

A. SOUTH SPIT is located on your left as you leave Willapa Bay. During ebb currents it generally breaks with swells 4 to 6 feet high. In addition to the danger of capsizing in this area, there is the added hazard of fouling your propeller on one of the many crab pot floats set by fishermen.

B. NORTH SPIT lies to your right as you leave Willapa Bay. This area is dangerous due to shallow water and there is generally an 8 to 10 foot swell running. During ebb currents it is usually breaking. Great caution should be used while fishing near this area as the drift rate is very fast and the turbulence may cause you to capsize.

BAR CONDITION REPORTS

Radio Station KAPA (1340 kHz) gives bar condition reports Monday through Saturday at 6:30 a.m., 9:00 a.m., 3:00 p.m., and 6:00 p.m., and on Sundays at 8:00 a.m., noon and 4:00 p.m.

GRAYS HARBOR BAR INFORMATION (See shaded areas on page 86.)

A. OUTER WHITCOMB FLATS is to your right as you leave Westport. This is a shoal area, and breakers sometimes exist, causing a dangerous situation.

B. THE MIDDLE GROUND is shoal water and a possible danger area where breakers are present. Stay to the south of this area when crossing the bar.

C. THE SOUTH JETTY is submerged from the exposed end to about 4,500 feet seaward. Usually the sunken rocks are not visible and the danger of grounding is always present. In other than very calm weather conditions breakers exist on the Sunken Jetty, creating the possibility of capsizing or grounding. The sunken or seaward end of the jetty is marked by a Lighted Buoy. Always avoid the area between Lighted Buoy and the raised or exposed end of the South Jetty. This area has caused most of the boating mishaps on the bar in recent years.

D. THE NORTH JETTY and the area north of it are dangerous because of shallow water and breaking surf.

ROUGH BAR WARNING SIGNS

A small boat rough bar advisory warning sign is located on the point of land Northwest of the Islander Motel and Restaurant. This sign faces 070° True.

BAR CONDITION REPORTS

Bar condition reports for Grays Harbor are given by the radio and television stations listed below:
KGHO—1200 kHz - Three times daily and when conditions change.
KXRO—1320 kHz - Three times daily and when conditions change.
TV—Channel 6 - (Local) - Continuous.

QUILLAYUTE RIVER BAR INFORMATION (See shaded areas on page 45.)

A. ROCK DIKE AND NORTH SIDE OF JAMES ISLAND: A rock dike, exposed at low water, runs from the northeastern side of James Island northeastward to the beach. It should be given a wide berth because of the danger of being swept upon it by river currents. The area northward of James Island is fouled with many submerged rocks and should be avoided.

B. OUTER END OF THE BREAKWATER: The end of the breakwater is slowly settling and the area around it is shoaling which causes breakers and should be avoided.

C. WASH ROCK: Wash Rock, 4 feet above water at mean low tide, lies about 55 feet off the southeast corner of James Island. In calm weather it can be passed fairly close, but care must be taken not to hit it. In rough weather there is considerable turbulence around it which will affect a boat's ability to maneuver.

D. AREA EAST OF BREAKWATER: This area is very shallow and breaks in almost all weather. It should be avoided.

QUILLAYUTE RIVER ENTRANCE

Quillayute River Entrance lies between James Island and a rock breakwater. The depth is about ten feet but is subject to extreme variations. The usual width at the entrance is about 70 feet. **While inside the entrance (north of the breakwater) stay on the jetty side of mid-channel and keep a sharp eye out for Indian fish nets especially between mid August and early June.** During the summer months there is very little danger of breakers on the bar except when a storm is passing through. The entrance to the river is hazardous after dark and entering should not be attempted unless one is familiar with the area. The entrance is marked by Quillayute River Direction Light which shows white, red, and green lights. The white light marks the centerline of the channel. If a mariner moves to the port or starboard side of the channel the white light will change to either red or green depending on which side of the channel the boat is tending toward (see the Coast Guard Light List, Volume VI, for a better description).

ROUGH BAR ADVISORY SIGNS

At Quillayute River the sign is mounted on the Northwest corner of the Coast Guard boathouse facing 016° True.

BAR CONDITION REPORTS

Bar condition reports for Quillayute River are given by Radio Station KVAC—1490 kHz. 6:00 a.m., 12:00 noon, 5:00 p.m. and when conditions change.

Entrance to the Columbia River: Bar Danger Areas

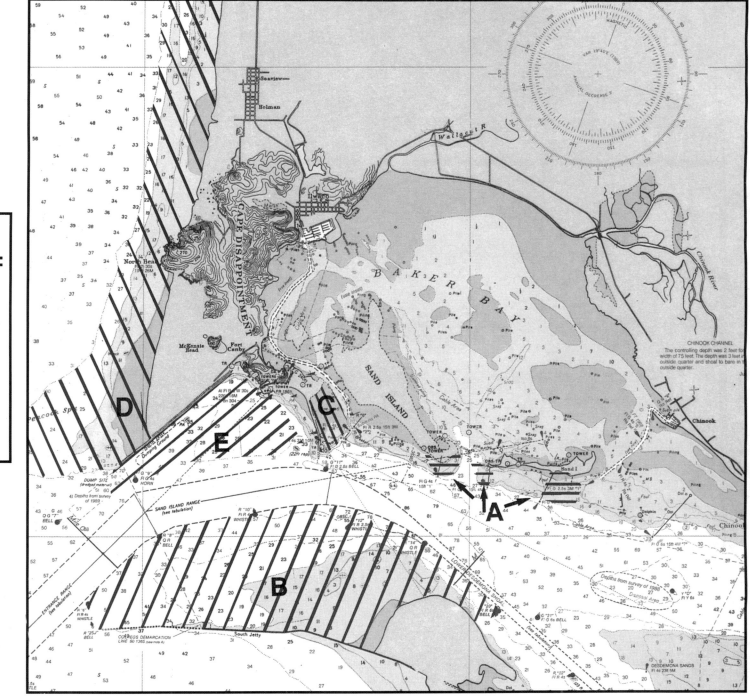

Columbia River Entrance: Bar Danger Areas

This chart is not intended for use in navigation.

A.* CHINOOK SPUR, UPPER, LOWER AND MIDDLE SAND ISLAND SPURS are built on two rows of staggered pilings. Currents flowing through these pilings attain a velocity of up to 5 knots. A boat which becomes disabled or is maneuvered in such a way as to come in contact with any of these spurs is almost sure to suffer damage. Even large boats have been capsized in these areas. Give these spurs a wide berth and never get close to them on the up-current side.

B.* CLATSOP SPIT is the most unpredictable area on the river entrance. During flood currents and slack water it may be calm with only a gentle swell breaking far in on the spit. Yet 5 or 10 minutes later, when the current has started to ebb, it can become extremely hazardous with breakers extending far out toward the channel. You should remain north of the red buoys in this area, particularly just before or during the ebb. The South Jetty has a section broken away on the outer end. The broken section is under water close to the surface. Boats should use extra caution in the area from the visible tip of the Jetty out to Nun Buoy "2SJ". Peacock and Clatsop Spits are called the graveyard of the Pacific for good reason.

C.* JETTY A which is southeast of Cape Disappointment, presents a particular danger when the current is ebbing. Water, flowing out of the river, is deflected by the jetty and frequently the current reaches 8 knots, often causing waves up to 8 feet high. Boats proceeding into Baker Bay West Channel make very little speed against the swift current and are exposed to the rough water or surf for long periods of time. The shallow sandy area should be avoided by small craft when heavy seas are present because of the surf which breaks on the beach.

D.* PEACOCK SPIT: Breakers are heavy in all types of current. Sports craft leaving the river should never be on the north side of the green buoys. When rounding Peacock Spit, give the breakers at least a half-mile clearance. Many times unusually large swells coming in from the sea suddenly commence breaking 1/4 to 1/2 miles outside the usual break on the end of the north jetty.

E.* MIDDLE GROUND: This is a shallow area between the North Jetty and main Ship Channel that is subject to breaking seas when swells as small as 4 feet are present. Conditons here can change in minutes with tidal current changes.

NO ROUGH BAR ADVISORY SIGN ESTABLISHED.

BAR CONDITION REPORTS
Radio Stations KVAS (1230 kHz) and KAST (1370 kHz) gives bar condition reports 15 minutes before and after the hour.

*See the red grids labeled A, B, C, D, & E on the above chart.